MW00577213

THE ENERGY BUS *for* SCHOOLS

7 **Ways** to Improve Your School Culture, Remove Negativity, Energize Your Teachers, and Empower Your Students

THE ENERGY BUS *for* SCHOOLS

JON GORDON

Bestselling Author of *The Energy Bus*

DR. JIM VAN ALLAN

President, Energy Bus for Schools

WILEY

Published by John Wiley & Sons, Inc., Hoboken, New Jersey.
Published simultaneously in Canada.

For general information on our other products and services or for technical support, please contact our Customer Care Department within the United States at (800) 762-2974, outside the United States at (317) 572-3993 or fax (317) 572-4002.

Wiley also publishes its books in a variety of electronic formats. Some content that appears in print may not be available in electronic formats. For more information about Wiley products, visit our web site at www.wiley.com.

Library of Congress Cataloging-in-Publication Data is Available:
ISBN 9781394233038 (Cloth)
ISBN 9781394233045 (ePub)
ISBN 9781394233052 (ePDF)

COVER DESIGN: PAUL MCCARTHY
COVER ART: © DAVID YOUNG-WOLFF / GETTY IMAGES

SKY10064817_011524

Contents

Preface

The desire to be a speaker and impact the world has been a driving force my entire life. In fourth and fifth grade, I entered and won our school's 4-H Public Speaking Contest with speeches about airplanes and then UFOs. In middle school, I gave an hour-long presentation on Australia, dressed in full costume. In high school, I won state and national public speaking competitions with some speeches written the night before. While the preparation part may not have been strong in my teenage years, my love of speaking was apparent to everyone. I would watch the keynote speaker at various conferences and wonder how I could be that person. At 17, as part of a time capsule project, I wrote that I would become a traveling speaker. That vision drove me to pursue opportunities in college that would allow my love of speaking to become a career.

In 2006, at my public relations internship, I still made it clear I wanted to be a speaker. People working there had just seen a speaker in Jacksonville and told me I should reach out to him. The speaker's name was Jon Gordon. My school, the University of Florida (Go Gators!), was just

90 minutes from Jacksonville. I was hesitant to reach out at first because I had tried in the past to connect with other speakers via email (this was pre–social media) and received nothing in reply. However, I sat down in my little apartment and fired off an email that would be a defining moment in my life. I wrote that I always wanted to be a speaker and would love to learn from Jon and ask him questions. I assumed no one would respond.

I assumed wrong, because the next day I woke up to an email reply in my inbox and there it was: a message from Jon Gordon. He said he would love to help and gave me his cell phone number. I called him that day, and for the next two hours, we spoke about life, speaking, and future goals. Jon was already challenging me to be goal-centered and create impactful messages. He offered me a handshake internship after the call. I hung up and celebrated in my room because my path had suddenly become very clear.

Soon after, Jon sent me an early version of a book he was getting published. I looked at the title on the Word document: *The Energy Bus*. We continued to work together on sales and marketing, and he offered me the opportunity to plan and manage his 30-city Energy Bus book tour. He received a sponsorship from a magazine that wrapped his SUV in Energy Bus colors and logos, as he drove from city to city promoting the book.

At 21 years old, I had no clue what I was doing (sorry, Jon, but it's true!). I was very early into my public relations studies, but, with the help of our business manager, Daniel Decker, I learned very quickly how to market and get people to the events. I was able to join Jon on the tour for the Midwest swing from Houston to Austin to Oklahoma City to Kansas and then Nebraska and Iowa before returning to Florida. Jon got food poisoning and was sick between Kansas and Nebraska so I had to drive the SUV. I like to proudly call myself the first "Energy Bus Driver" because I was literally driving the Energy Bus on the tour. The tour had its ups and downs, but the book would explode on the scene in the coming years. If you are reading this book, there's a good chance you started with *The Energy Bus* at some point.

I have wanted to write a book since I met Jon in 2006. We all set goals for ourselves, and this was high on my list. I have worked primarily with schools since I met Jon and earned my PhD in educational leadership. For my dissertation, I studied the impact of an early version of the Energy Bus for Schools program in 2017. Energy Bus has been part of my life for almost two decades. From the first Energy Bus book tour, to writing my PhD dissertation, to working with hundreds of school leaders and educators and now leading our Energy Bus for Schools program, I know it was part of my life plan to write this book with Jon Gordon and share the 7 steps to energize your school culture. Just like I am living my dream now as a speaker and author, your dream culture is just ahead. I am excited and grateful you are looking to improve your school culture and making the Energy Bus part of that process. Thank you for riding this bus.

—Dr. Jim Van Allan

Introduction

If you picked up this book and have not read *The Energy Bus* first, the following is a short description of what that book is all about.

It's Monday morning and George walks out the front door to his car and a flat tire. But this is the least of his problems. His home life is in shambles and his team at work is in disarray. With a big new product launch coming up in two weeks, he has to find a way to get it together or risk losing his marriage and job. Forced to take the bus to work, George meets a unique kind of bus driver and an interesting set of characters (passengers) that over the course of two weeks share the 10 rules for the ride of his life—and attempt to help him turn around his work and team and save his job and marriage from almost inevitable destruction.

The Energy Bus has now gone on to sell over three million copies worldwide since it was published in 2007. Many schools nationwide have used *The Energy Bus* in various forms for a book study, workshop, keynote, and most powerfully through our Certified Energy Bus for Schools program. It's a transformative book that gives readers a roadmap for how to overcome negativity in their work and lives. No one goes through life untested, but the answer is to always stay positive with a spirit of vision, trust, and optimism. *The Energy Bus* is a story that educators find relevant to their situation, no matter when or why they read it. It's a book that has inspired our school-based program and led to this new book. We encourage you to read the original *The Energy Bus* book at some point and continue to create the best ride of your life!

Chapter 1

7 Steps to Improve Your School Culture

It's an ongoing process to improve your school culture. School leaders should always look for ways to improve, retool, and grow as time goes on. This is a process that involves multiple steps and a lot of intentionality and purpose. The process to improve your school culture begins with inviting your staff on the bus.

Set the vision for the school and invite them to be part of it. Encourage them to join you on the Energy Bus. The team is the star when it comes to making a school vision a reality. It will take a group effort, and people need to be invited to be part of it.

Once the team is on the bus, your vision can be realized. The next step is building a positive culture. Everyone in the building understands they are part of the culture, and they help create it. The Energy Bus principles provide pillars of strength that help you build your foundation. These principles mean something to each person and act as a unifying agent. Staff and students now have a common language and go through a common experience that creates a common bond. The Energy Bus truly helps you create a positive and strong school culture.

The next step in improvement is to fuel your ride with positive energy. Mindset and mentality are two driving factors in staff, students, and school leadership. The Energy Bus teaches everyone how to develop a positive mindset and perspective and how to fuel themselves and others with positivity. This will create resilience in the face of challenges, change, and negativity. This also improves morale and performance in a big way!

With your vision set and positive mindset in place, it's important to realize that schools are in the positive people business. Human beings need to be nurtured, loved, guided, supported, and encouraged. In a high-pressure career like education, the next step in improving school culture is to love your passengers so your staff and students want to be "on the bus", feel like they are part of the process and share love along the way. This is all about finding unique ways to show love to students and staff, which helps them to build strong relationships in the process. We share many great ideas in this book.

No matter how much love and unity you have, negativity will still find a way in. In order to improve a school culture, school leaders and staff cannot be afraid to confront negativity and work to transform it. Negativity, whining, gossiping, and complaining will not go away without precaution and intervention strategies. A strategic plan with a positive campus culture will help school leaders looking to manage negativity and turn it into positive energy. We look forward to sharing many ideas with you in this book.

Once negativity has been transformed and more people are on the bus, it's time to refuel, reenergize, and refocus your passengers. It's all about purpose which is the ultimate fuel for a positive campus culture and is essential in avoiding burnout. Knowing your *why* and understanding how it helps enhance a positive campus culture is key. When you face tough times, refocusing your staff and students on their purpose and positive mindset will help them to become resilient and productive problem-solvers and communicators.

In the end, the process to improve your school culture is about bringing people together with a shared mission. The goal is to create a fleet of bus drivers. This fleet will do amazing and inspiring things on campus. The fleet will also take the positive messages into their communities and into the lives of your staff and students' families. Everyone connected to this fleet of bus drivers will be positively impacted.

The rest of the book explores the 7 steps in greater detail:

- Invite Your Staff on the Bus
- Build a Positive Culture
- Fuel Your Ride with Positive Energy
- Love Your Passengers

- Transform Negativity
- Refuel, Reenergize, and Refocus with Purpose
- Create a Fleet of Bus Drivers

Get ready to improve your school culture with real stories, turnkey strategies, best practices, and research as you enjoy the ride of your life!

Chapter 2

Invite Your Staff on the Bus

"Remember, you're driving the bus, George," Joy said. "But as you drive you want to keep asking people to get on. The worst they can say is no. If you don't ask, they won't know to get on. Plus, the more people you pick up along the way, the more energy you create during your ride. The goal is to eventually have a standing room only bus and since this is an energy bus it is always expanding so you'll always be able to add more people."

—*The Energy Bus*, page 56

We are often asked to define the key to a successful school, the kind of school where every teacher wants to teach and every parent wants to send their kids. The simple answer is culture.

It's easy to diagnose a school's culture when we walk through the entrance for a training. What feeling do we get as outsiders coming into the school? Are there friendly faces to greet us in the office and show us where to go?

Do we see bulletin boards of the Energy Bus or other positive messages on walls made by teachers immensely more creative than us? Can we imagine our own children attending this school? Culture is not one thing; it is everything and it requires everyone. To build a great culture you must invite your team on the bus and get them to work as a team.

No One Creates Success Alone

Creating a positive school culture is a collective process. It requires a unified staff where everyone wants to contribute to the school's success. One of the most important jobs of a school leader is creating and managing relationships. Great leaders must hire the right people and then build and develop those relationships on the journey. One person cannot continuously drive a positive culture. Trying to do so leads to burnout. The key is to build a team that creates success together—and have more fun on the bus—as you pursue excellence.

In rural Kansas sits USD 216 Deerfield Schools, one of our first Certified Energy Bus Schools. I (Jim) completed a training for them at the beginning of the school year to "get them on the bus." They had a new superintendent who wanted to start out his tenure on a positive note. It was a successful workshop. Months went by and I had not heard from Deerfield. I hardly saw Energy Bus for

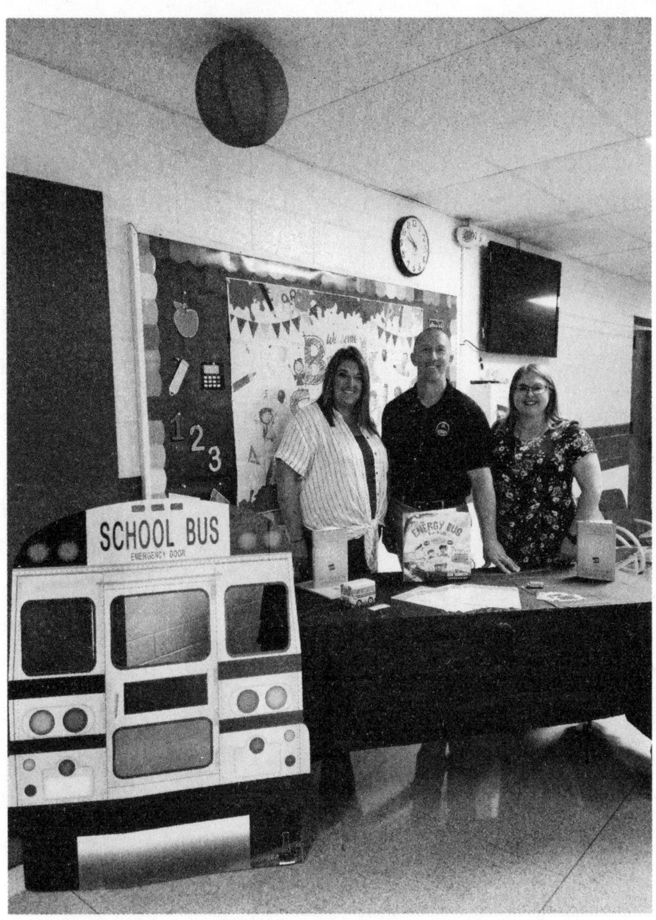

Deerfield Schools in Kansas back on the Energy Bus.

Schools pictures on our Facebook group or on their own social media.

I reached out during the school year, and their superintendent said Year 1 was not going as planned. He took ownership and said he didn't build a team. He didn't invite his staff on the bus. He decided to renew their certification, do things differently, and follow my guidance and create a team effort and a more collective approach. They hired a second counselor, and she teamed up with their existing counselor to help implement the program. I was invited back out to Kansas to reenergize the staff and stress the value of teamwork to make the Energy Bus for Schools program a success on their campus.

After meeting with both their counselors, it was obvious their Energy Bus ride this year was going be a great one. They had a plan in place to fully engage with faculty and students. They also had excitement and enthusiasm. They wanted Deerfield Schools to have a positive and engaged culture. They saw themselves as a true team and knew they had to invite the staff on the bus to be successful. Deerfield Schools has become a model Energy Bus School. Their counselors continue to work hard to create a unified culture where everyone wants to succeed. They work closely with the superintendent and faculty members to make the Energy Bus for Schools program fun and engaging for all. They are on the bus and working as a team.

Inviting People on the Bus

A school staff is comprised of people from different generations, backgrounds, ethnicities, and experience levels. Schools leaders must invite all their staff on the bus.

Aventura Charter School in Miami rides the Energy Bus.

While some staff may seem skeptical at first, it is a school leader's responsibility to show them how they are part of the team.

With veteran staff members, school leaders must explain why this time will be different. With newer staff members, more guidance and direction is needed. Trust is essential for everyone to get on. Staff members will not get on the bus automatically; they need to be invited on the bus.

Many of our Energy Bus Schools find creative ways to invite staff on the bus. They print bus tickets from our website, EnergyBusSchools.com, personalize them with staff members' names, and distribute them before school starts. Staff may find a bus ticket in their mailbox, hanging from their door, or even hand-delivered by an excited school leader.

School leaders then ask each staff member to bring their ticket to the first staff meeting and turn them in with a signature. Often these bus tickets go on display for all to see. These initial staff meetings are a shared experience for a new school year. They are tone setters and should be treated as such. It's a tribal experience where leadership is saying to their team, "I want you to be part of this."

Shared Experience

There is something truly powerful about a group of people going through a shared experience. Everyone tends to feel more bonded because they all have something in common. This explains why it is so important for families to spend time with each other because relationships grow through shared experiences. In a 2009 research article titled "What Works in Professional Development?" from

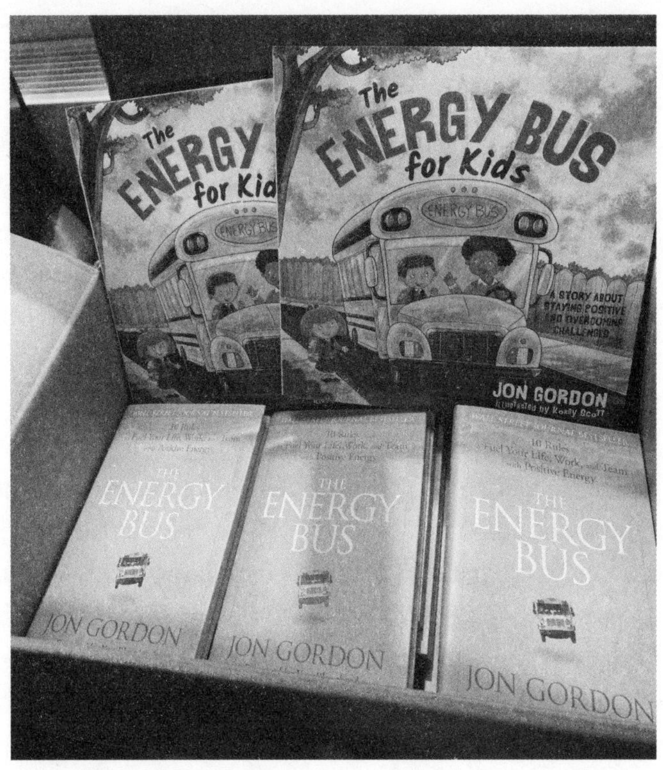

An Energy Bus School inviting their staff "on the bus" with new books for the school year.

The Leading Edge, Thomas Guskey and Kwang Suk Yoon indicated that the "most effective way to bring improvement in a school is to have educators in each school meet regularly to explore common problems and seek solutions based on shared experiences and collective wisdom." Staff members feel a sense of belonging and pride in accomplishing something together.

This is why staff members need to be invited on the bus and make a personal commitment to the team. Whether this is through the bus ticket activity, signing a vision statement banner, or doing a staff field trip or party, the shared experience is key. No one can hide or let others do the work. The Energy Bus for Schools program has been a huge success because every staff member commits to the process. They believe in the principles from the Energy Bus, which will become the foundation for their school culture.

People bond over a feeling of unity and togetherness. When they make those bonds public through some type of commitment act, it is even more powerful. Staff members are active participants in the culture-building process when they put their name on a bus ticket, do a presentation on an Energy Bus rule to the whole group, or even share a meal together. They are in essence saying "I am part of this team." When your staff gets on the bus together, they are ready to make a positive impact as ONE!

Share the Vision and Purpose

As a school leader, now that you have invited your staff on the bus and have generated commitment from your team, it is time to share the vision and purpose of why The Energy Bus will work on campus and how it will drive your school culture. Many schools have made the positive choice to become Certified Energy Bus Schools. They join an extensive network of schools all linked by the common goal of creating a positive campus culture. These schools share a love and admiration for the principles from *The Energy Bus* book. More than just a theme, these principles become a foundation for your school culture.

For many schools, it is a natural fit. Waimalu Elementary, in Hawaii, saw the Energy Bus as a natural next step. Their former principal, Glen Iwamoto, who is now working in a district-level position, mentioned how their school vision is to "develop character, attitudes, and skills to excel in a global society." He sees the Energy Bus rules as supporting his vision because they help to build a positive attitude and strong character within the students. He was able to successfully share his vision with his staff, bring in workshops, and join the Energy Bus for Schools program.

The Energy Bus for Schools program contains activity guides and other resources to positively impact students, staff, and even parents and community members. My (Jim's) dissertation research from 2017 showed one of the number-one factors from the program is the common language used by everyone at the school. Students and staff use the terminology from the book such as "fuel your ride with positive energy" and "love your passengers." Common language like this builds bonds between people. Schools inside this program create a shared experience for all who are on the bus.

Spirit Lake Elementary, in Iowa, explained that finding a program to fit the needs of more than 70 staff members and align with their school vision was difficult. They

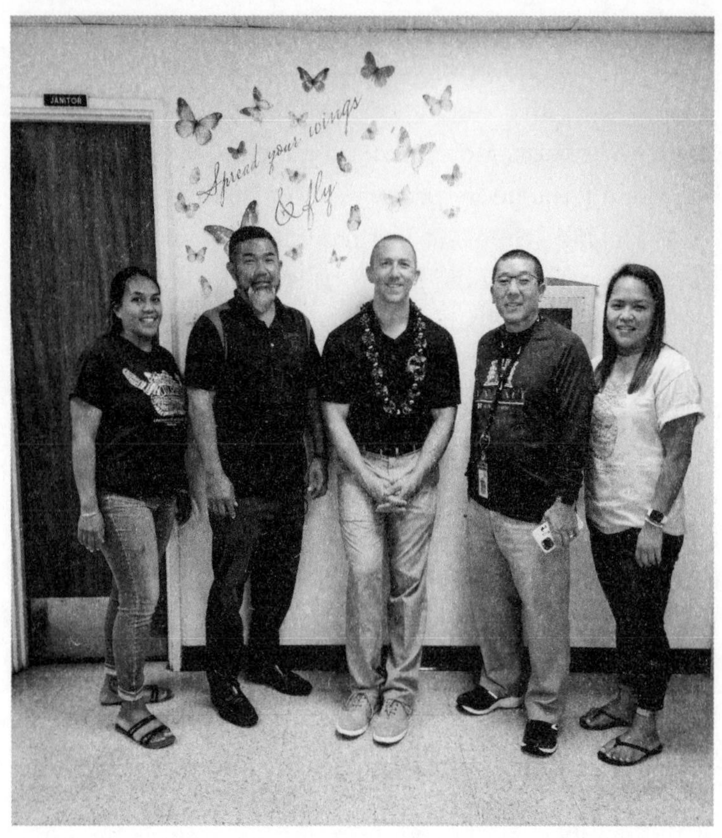

conducted a survey of their staff needs and found teachers asked for a program with common language, goals, and beliefs. They joined the Energy Bus for Schools program and see it as a great fit because the principles align with their culture playbook. They mentioned how having fun, with a unified vision and common language, makes Spirit Lake the kind of place you want to work and send your children to. This is the definition of a destination location.

Waimalu and Makalapa Elementary Schools in Hawaii are on the Energy Bus.

Leaders set the tone and share the vision. That is a big part of their job. School leaders need to share the vision for what they want the school to be in order to get them on the bus. When you invite your team on the bus, also share the vision to your staff in a fun and interactive way and help them to see the impact they can and will make. This will cause them to want to get on the bus and be a part of a school that makes a difference. Many staff members have seen school visions come and go due to a lack of consistency and accountability. They may be the ones less likely to get on the bus right away. That's why it's important to state up front that this is different. We are not doing a "one and done" workshop and training. This is not just a theme. This is an ongoing process. Share your vision with heart, enthusiasm, and passion.

Inviting Your Leadership Team

A big part of inviting your school on the bus is inviting your leadership team on the bus to help you lead and improve your culture. In my (Jim's) experience leading the Energy Bus for Schools program, I often communicate directly with many assistant principals, counselors, and others on the leadership team at schools. You can sense their real passion and energy to create and work in a positive school. Many times, these individuals are the ones who have read *The Energy Bus* and bring it to the attention of their principals. The leadership team at a school consist of the key bus drivers who will make your school a success.

At the Villages Charter School, in Florida, they have a strong leadership team that is actively driving the Energy Bus. They have over 2,100 students across multiple campuses in one of the fastest-growing regions in Florida. Their director of education, Dr. Randy McDaniel, made sure to empower his building principals to drive the bus with passion and energy. From the beginning, Dr. McDaniel invited his leadership team on the bus and now they are one of our strongest districts.

Fun Ways to Invite Your Staff on the Bus

Inviting staff on the bus doesn't have to be serious. You can make it fun and eventful. For example, West Lyon Elementary, in Iowa, decided to take a unique approach to inviting their staff on the Energy Bus. They held one of their first staff meetings off-site and created a mini-competition to introduce the 10 rules from the book. Each Energy Bus rule had its own station where staff had to complete a task, learn the rule, and move on. One of the stations included nailing things together to illustrate "You're the Driver of Your Bus" by "driving" a nail into wood (do this at your discretion). They had a frisbee toss for inviting others on the bus and filled up water jugs for fueling your ride with positive energy. By mixing a traditional staff meeting and activities, the leadership team showed the staff the fun power of the Energy Bus. They also showed the staff positive possibilities.

Another one of our Energy Bus Schools literally invited the staff on a bus. After an engaging meeting where the principal handed out copies of *The Energy Bus* to everyone, they boarded a school bus. The staff drove through the neighborhoods where their students live to see life from their perspective. The principal wanted the staff to understand the environment in which their students live and realize just how important the Energy Bus could be in creating a positive environment for students growing up in a difficult environment.

While a field trip is not a requirement to invite others on the bus and share the vision, it can be a fun way to engage with the staff. If using a traditional meeting on campus, be sure to hand out *The Energy Bus* book to everyone. Ask key staff members and the leadership team to present different rules from the book. As part of the Energy Bus for Schools program, there is even a video of Jon Gordon teaching the rules from a school's perspective. Be clever with engagement to show the staff that it is more fun on the bus then waiting at the bus stop.

Improving school culture is not easy, and the challenges are real inside our schools. Staff shortages, stress, and negativity are present and, if left unchecked, can create a toxic culture. The effects of negativity on campus are real. Schools need to do their best to invite everyone on the bus and create a positive school culture. When school leaders do this, they are well positioned to take on the negativity and challenges as a team that you will read more about in this book. No one creates success alone, and when schools get on the bus together, they are on their way to creating a positive future.

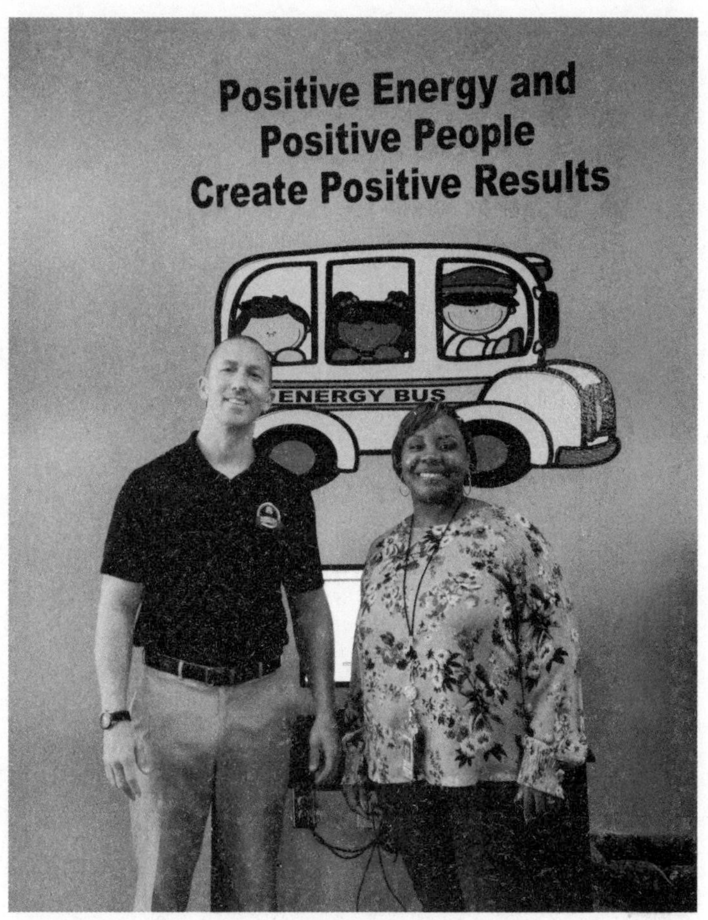

Dr. Jim Van Allan with Dr. Marchelle Hasan, principal at Saddleback Elementary in Arizona. She wants the caption on the wall to be her school's vision.

19

Invite Your Staff on the Bus

Chapter 3

Build a Positive Culture

"Like a successful rock band where each member plays a different instrument that magically contributes to an incredible sound, each member of George's team was playing their parts, and the music was perfect. They were energized, synchronized, and fast becoming a team. They were on George's bus together with a shared vision, shared purpose, and a collective powerful force of positive energy all focused in the same direction."

—*The Energy Bus*, page 136

Building a positive culture is a journey that takes time, effort, and a lot of intentionality. This may be the main reason why you are reading this book. Earlier, we established the importance of creating a positive vision and inviting others to be on your bus. One of the main themes from the previous chapter is "no one creates success alone." Creating a culture is everyone's job. Everyone creates the culture, and the culture impacts everyone. According to data from *IBIS World and Public School Review*, the average school in 2023 has about 70 employees and 514 students. The average school culture is impacting close to 600 people daily. Some high schools in Texas, Florida, and California have enrollments higher than 4,000 students.

These numbers demonstrate the urgency and importance of building a school culture. The students connected to a school will take the lessons and habits they learn into the real world. As they enter the workforce, potentially start families, and live in a community, they will remember the impact of their school culture. Maya Angelou famously said, "I've learned that people will forget what you said, people will forget what you did, but people will never forget how you made them feel." Students will always remember how they felt at school and this will impact their well-being and future decisions as to where they send their children to school. The character of our students can be shaped by the culture of a school.

The National Center for Analysis of Longitudinal Data in Education Research found that 500,000 teachers are leaving the profession annually. Even before Covid-19, teacher shortages were seen as a major challenge by districts. While some teachers leave because of retirement, this was only a small percentage of the 500,000. A toxic culture is to blame for many people wanting out.

Nationally, across all jobs, the United States saw 24 million people leave their jobs in 2021. Research from MIT shows two driving factors behind this "Great Resignation." First, a toxic culture is a main reason for people leaving their jobs across the board. A second factor is a failure to recognize performance of employees. By looking at the suggestions and examples from this chapter, a school can begin the process of flipping the script to retain good teachers and staff. While they are on campus, they need to be engaged, recognized, appreciated, and included in the culture-building process.

Culture impacts the staff and their well being too. A staff that creates and works in a positive culture will be happier and more energized about their work and life than in a negative culture. When a staff knows they have the power to create their culture and are a key part of the process, their energy will rise. Culture always starts at the top with the leader and then it comes to life with input from everyone in the school. The leader sets the tone.

One such leader resides in a small town in Texas with a population of 1,643. Dr. Teddy Clevenger is the superintendent of Bartlett ISD, and he is on a mission to build a positive school culture. I (Jim) had the pleasure of meeting him and speaking to his district in August 2023. Recently, the city of Bartlett was seeing an exodus of people due to a failing school district and a losing football team. Bartlett ISD was an F district in Texas and was having a hard time building any momentum for growth.

Enter Dr. Clevenger. In a matter of four years, he has turned the tide in Bartlett. After assembling what he feels is the "best leadership team in the state," he and the team are on a mission to rebuild the district literally and figuratively, and they have changed the mentality of all stakeholders within the district. He knew he had to get the right people "on the bus" and teach them to believe in his turnaround vision. Due to his hands-on leadership style, vision, and ability to get much-needed resources to his district, they are on the rise and approaching an A grade in Texas.

It's a remarkable turnaround for a district that people had stopped believing in. However, that's not the end of the story. Dr. Clevenger worked extremely hard to pass a $20 million bond for the district. It took two separate votes, but the community finally believed in his mission, vision, and direction to change the culture in Bartlett. The biggest question the community had for him was "How long are you staying?" They must have liked his response because the bond finally passed. Bartlett ISD will now be receiving a full facelift as they build for new growth into the area. Instead of people fleeing the town, it is coming back to life. I asked Dr. Clevenger why he took the job when it was not

Dr. Jim Van Allan with the school leaders in Bartlett ISD.

viewed as an attractive position. He said he was "by nature a builder and liked to fix things." In what is probably the biggest project of his life, he is rebuilding a once great district that had fallen on hard times into a destination district again.

In 2023, Dr. Clevenger wanted to further elevate the district and he embraced the Energy Bus. The staff is doing a full book study and they are on their way to becoming a Certified Energy Bus District. He knows building a positive culture is not easy but is worth the process.

Dr. Jim Van Allan with Dr. Teddy Clevenger of Bartlett ISD.

Know What You Stand For

Culture doesn't happen by accident. To build a great culture, you must know what you stand for. When I (Jon) speak to schools, I always ask what they stand for and someone always says "students." I believe everyone stands for students so I encourage them to reinforce this belief.

If you happen to get hired at Benton County Schools, a district in rural Tennessee, you may get a surprise on your first day. They commit to giving every new hire a copy of *The Energy Bus* book. In Benton County, the Energy Bus is not just a theme but part of their cultural foundation and identity. The book is read by staff and teachers on all levels and discussed throughout the year. I (Jim) spoke here in 2022, and it is apparent this district is fully on the bus. They have clear expectations and guidelines for how to build a positive culture. Most importantly, they know what they stand for, and it is the 10 Energy Bus principles.

In my (Jim's) dissertation research on the Energy Bus for Schools program, I studied one of the first schools that enrolled in the program. Their principal made it clear that they intended to avoid complacency and focus on improving overall staff morale at the school. They stood for excellence and it made a huge difference with their culture and performance. Waimalu Elementary, in Hawaii, is all about culture and excellence, and they live by the saying "culture beats strategy every time." In the previous chapter, you read about Principal Glen Iwamoto's vision to "develop the character, attitude, and skills to excel in a global society." Glen told us their school works toward creating a warm and welcoming environment for everyone, and this helps them achieve their vision.

Everything that Waimalu is doing is connected and links back to a desire to build a positive culture. They know that culture beats strategy every time because the best plans are pointless without the staff nurturing the appropriate culture. If they want to achieve their vision of developing students and getting them ready to be part of a community, they must invest in the relationships and morale on campus. We will talk more about this in the "Love Your Passengers" chapter. These feelings and campus environment have a direct impact on students and staff. It created an environment where everyone feels welcome and ready to contribute to the school's success. They are a school that has a flexible plan, but more importantly a desire to create a positive and welcoming campus every single day. It's what they stand for. If your school is struggling or perhaps you are dealing with a lot of negativity and challenges, it's always best to get back to the fundamentals and make sure everyone knows what they stand for.

Knowing what you stand for makes every decision easier. It also makes hiring easier, because when you hire people who stand for what your school stands for and also fit your culture, they will live, breathe, and carry out your vision and mission.

Set Expectations

It is essential that school leaders communicate these expectations, reinforce them, put initiatives into practice, and be consistent with them. When you know what you stand for, you can set expectations and standards that ensure your staff and students build your culture the right way.

South Conway Elementary, in South Carolina, is a place I (Jim) have spoken to virtually and in person. Their principal, Leon Hayes, has been in education for over three decades. He believes very little negativity exists on campus mainly because they have established a strong, student-centered culture that prevents the negativity from rooting. He and his staff have been focused on culture for a while. He has set the expectations and everyone rises up to meet these expectations. From time to time there are staff members who do not like change or have opposing viewpoints in school direction. However, their leadership team makes a consistent effort to check in with staff members weekly to discuss or resolve any negativity that could be present. While we are going to discuss ways to transform negativity in schools, keep in mind that it starts with creating the right culture.

South Conway has a culture that is strong and everyone knows what they stand for, so negativity doesn't breed and grow here. Leon says it is critical that you get the right people on the bus. He says they hire well, thoroughly check references, and get to know the candidate prior to and during the interview. They are not just filling a teaching or staff position with just anyone; it has to be the right person for their culture.

Dr. Jim Van Allan with South Conway Elementary Principal Leon Hayes.

Know Your Core Values

When a school knows what it stands for, this becomes the foundation. For many schools it is the 10 Energy Bus principles. For others, it may be a vision and mission statement, list of words, or something different. When you know what you stand for, decisions are easier to make. Everything from hiring to school events to programs can be dictated by your values. Schools must find ways to live and breathe their core values.

At Spirit Lake Elementary, in Iowa, Principal Kasey Huebner said their main core value is relationship building. He knows relationships are the foundation for everything they want to accomplish. As a Certified Energy Bus School, the staff has experienced the power that positivity had on their vision, teamwork, and relationships on campus. By focusing on relationships, they strengthen their culture, mission, and each other. Core values come to life when everyone involved with your culture knows what they are and ingrains in them who they are and what they are expected to do each day.

A big part of the leader's job is to remind everyone what the core values are so they can make sure to consistently focus on them and live and breathe what they stand for.

Spirit Lake put together their "One Word" vision statements in the shape of a giant school bus for all to see. The "One Word" activity is an easy and effective way to pick a single concept on which to focus during the school year. Many goals and strategies will stem from this one word collaboration. Spirit Lake had students and staff write their words

Spirit Lake made their "One Word" vision statements into a huge school bus to inspire everyone.

on a piece of printer paper and arranged into the shape of a bus. Nancy Kriener, the instructional coach at the school, mentioned how this central piece became a daily reminder of their vision, culture, values, and what they stand for.

Bring Core Values to Life

Spirit Lake's example of "One Words" in the shape of the bus is one way to connect what you stand for with tangible reminders that help you create positive habits and bring your core values to life. After all, the key to creating a great culture is to bring the core values you write on the walls to life in the hearts and minds of your staff and students. Our Certified Energy Bus Schools are some of the most creative schools out there in the ways they bring their culture to life. We highly recommend that you share your core values on the walls and accent the decor of the school. It should be obvious to anyone who visits the campus what the school values. Every time a student walks through the halls, they should see and feel the core values. What we see and experience daily play large roles in what we think about and become. The mind is a pivotal tool to dictate success and should be nurtured and reinforced with positive symbolism all around us.

Walk into Central Boulevard Elementary, in Bethpage, New York, and you'll be greeted by a large cutout yellow Energy Bus. Often there are student and administrator pictures as the passengers. Student vision statements, "One Words," and core values are written all over the bus for everyone to see. In 2021, outgoing Principal Steve Furrey wanted to bring in the Energy Bus program as one of his last legacies on campus. There was a commitment to continue the program after he retired. Steve wanted everyone on campus to know what Central Boulevard stands for, and that is positivity. You will see Energy Bus quotes, buses, and other road-related decor around campus. They are constant reminders to stay positive and focus on positive relationships.

I (Jim) spoke at Meadow View Elementary in North Carolina, and the principal took me on a tour of the campus. I looked up in their main entrance area and saw all the Energy Bus rules printed on fun banners, and hanging

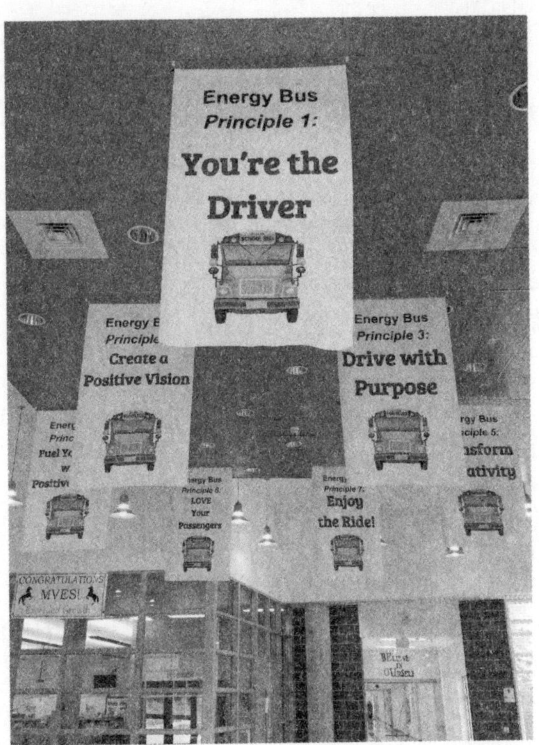

Meadow View Elementary in North Carolina filled the entrance with Energy Bus banners.

from the ceiling. Every person walking around campus can look up and see what the school stands for.

This is one of the keys to the Energy Bus program: we help to bring core values to life. Decor, cutout buses, and Energy Bus quotes on the walls are pivotal, but let's remember that core values on walls isn't enough. Schools can live and breathe their core values through assemblies, songs, announcements, and staff meetings.

For example, anytime I have a school assembly with elementary students, we sing one of the Energy Bus songs, to the tune of "B-I-N-G-O." It teaches the students to be the drivers of their bus, have a vision, and don't bully. It's a catchy song that will definitely be stuck in their head.

Another way our schools live their core values is by showcasing student work and recognizing "Energy Bus Drivers of the Month." This allows them to reinforce the culture and behaviors they want to see. Schools cannot expect a mission statement or poster to be lived if it is not being reinforced. The "Energy Bus Driver of the Month" aspect of the program allows teachers to recognize students who best exemplified that month's Energy Bus rule. In the program, schools focus on one of the five main Energy Bus rules at a time. It can be a student who was most engaged in discussions and activities or the one who best lived that principle. Teachers should also verbally reinforce the behaviors they want to see. Most schools will recognize their Drivers of the Month as part of a large school assembly, whether virtual or in person. Some of our schools use the power of closed-circuit announcements if they don't have the space to bring everyone together for an assembly. They will broadcast directly into all the classrooms. Recognizing students in front of their peers has a lasting impact. The mascot at my sons' elementary school is the Wildcat and their core values are Polite, Aware, Wise, and Safe (PAWS). Each classroom gives out a PAWSome Wildcat Award each week to recognize the students who are regularly being polite, aware, wise, and safe. The classes make a big deal of the presentation, and the winner gets to do show-and-tell all week. It is a big badge of honor in the elementary school community. The teachers do a great job reinforcing why PAWS is important and how to live by it. Most importantly, the school is reinforcing the behaviors they want to see from students in a fun and public manner.

The Symbolism of the Energy Bus

If you look at the word "culture" through definition standards, it is the "behaviors, beliefs, and traditions and their shared meaning that guides the standards of the group." The important words in that definition are "shared meaning." One of the main points from the last chapter is a shared experience our schools go through when they are in the Energy Bus program. The activities, language, and symbols truly impact every person, even the parents. We often have many newer principals decide to turn their schools into Certified Energy Bus Schools because they are looking for a way to start to build a culture. If the previous principal did not leave a roadmap or the school in an ideal position, the new principal must work to develop traditions, habits, beliefs, and symbols that everyone believes, lives, and shares.

After 2020, many schools flocked our way because their identity was lost during the pandemic years, when a lot of culture and relationship-building priorities were put on hold in order to focus solely on safety regulations and health protocols. We helped them reestablish their identity and create symbols that help strengthen their culture for years to come and serve as an unshakable foundation.

Cultural symbols allow a group that shares the same beliefs to identify and celebrate those beliefs with these symbols. Think about the flag of a country or logo of a sports team. People have a unified belief when they see these symbols and it reminds them what they mean and stand for.

I (Jim) spoke at Dorie Miller Intermediate School in Texas in 2018. They were embarking on Year 2 inside the Energy Bus program and wanted additional training for the staff. As I pulled into the school parking lot, it was obvious they were an Energy Bus School. Positioned near the front entrance was a decommissioned school bus with the words "Energy Bus" painted on the side. There were also paintings of students happily riding the bus. This is a school that rode the Energy Bus for many years and experienced a plethora of positive success. The symbolism of the actual bus parked in front of the school is a constant reminder to celebrate what they stand for and keep driving toward the future.

Dorie Miller is not the only school using an actual school bus. Dayton City Schools in Tennessee surprised their staff with an "Energy Bus" that pulled up for a photo op after one of my (Jim's) speaking engagements. Their superintendent had been fixing up an old bus for

An actual Energy Bus parked outside Dorie Miller Intermediate School in Texas.

years and decided to surprise her staff. It symbolized the journey the district was about to take using the Energy Bus as their guide. These symbols show a commitment to culture and, in turn, create a common bond and experience.

In April 2022, I (Jim) embarked on an Energy Bus for Schools tour across the country. The goal was to meet as many educators and administrators as possible. I wanted to give these schools the tools, resources, and strategies to build a positive school. We were fortunate to have host schools in each city we attended. Outside Houston, we stopped at Heritage Elementary. This school had previously worked with *The Energy Bus* book and principles. Many times a school will do a book study with *The Energy Bus* book. Some will schedule a training to accompany it and others will use our Field Guide and other online resources to bring it to life on campus.

Heritage was happy to host our tour stop and had several fun items to show me. Each year they decorate a ceiling tile to show their focused theme for the year, and they took me to a classroom that featured an Energy

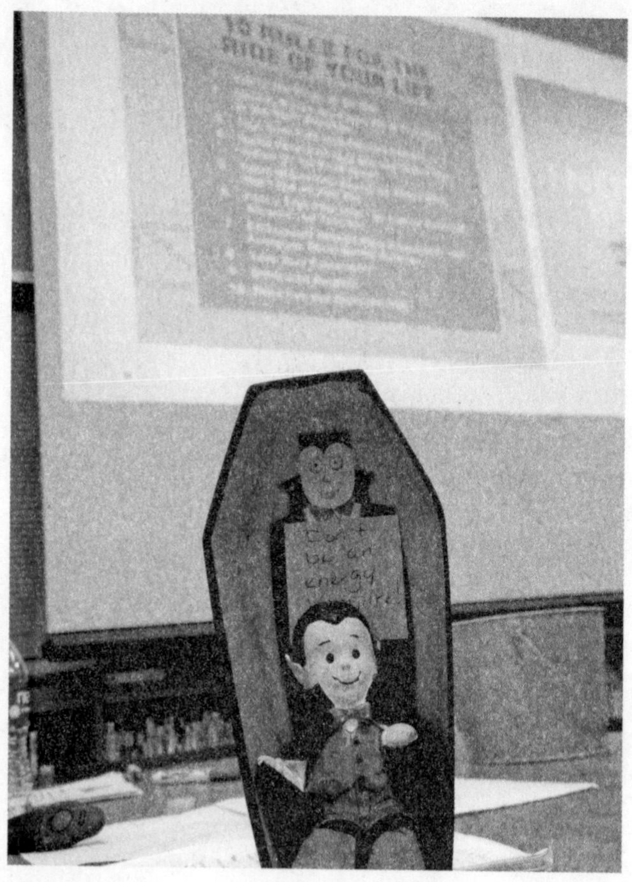

You never want this "energy vampire" to appear on your desk at Heritage Elementary in Texas.

Bus ceiling tile. This tile in particular reminded staff and students that with the Energy Bus, "this is how we roll." They also brought out a small vampire doll they used as a symbol for being an energy vampire. You never wanted this energy vampire doll to appear in your box or in your classroom! Years after they introduced the Energy Bus to campus, it continues to impact them with the symbols they created. It helped them to remember the Energy Bus principles that still guide them.

Symbols are something that can stand the test of time. If used appropriately and consistently, they can allow a culture to create and celebrate its shared meaning and connection for a long time. It also reinforces characteristics and behaviors you want to see more of, or get rid of energy vampires like you see in this picture.

Consistency Creates Culture

Whatever culture you are creating and values you are sharing and bringing to life with symbols, it's important to be consistent. Culture is not a one time thing. It's an all the time mission.

At Jensen Beach High School in Florida, Principal Lori Vogel has a mission of creating a positive and energized campus. She wanted the start of the 2023–2024 school year to feel different this time. As most great leaders have an attention to detail, she knew the announcements were a good place to start. In the past, the announcements were simply pointing out all the rules being broken and did not add much value. Now, she uses the morning announcements as a way of complimenting her students and staff, pointing out positive things she sees and hears, and motivating them each morning. Additionally, she is encouraging her staff to have more positive body language and bring positive energy to the campus every day. They are actively using The Energy Bus terminology in staff meetings too. Her consistency with this new vision for a positive campus culture is working well. She is reporting positive feedback from staff, and Jensen Beach was just named one of the top 100 high schools in the state of Florida.

It all starts with positive habits, which lead to positive results. When students consistently hear the meaning of various Energy Bus principles on the announcements, see things on the walls, and talk about them in their classrooms, those values and culture come to life. The key is to be consistent the whole time. Spirit Lake Elementary has been one of our most consistent and engaged schools. This is a strong testament to their leaders Kasey Huebner and Nancy Kriener, who continue to pour into their culture. They mention how Spirit Lake implements directed activities that focus on and reinforce the Energy Bus principles. They want students to see that their actions and choices impact others. They do a terrific job not letting apathy or complacency enter their buildings.

Mt. Washington Middle School, in Kentucky, operates the same way. Principal Tim Ridley knows that culture is how a school feels when you walk into the building. He says that even with great academic instruction, if there is a negative culture, the school will never reach its full potential. Tim does a remarkable job, consistently connecting with students where they are, even through a school-sponsored TikTok account. Tim will dance his way through the day on TikTok if it means his students will smile and have a better attitude. His methods make him approachable, which is a huge plus with middle school students. Tim understands the concept of consistency in building a positive campus culture.

When school leaders and teachers connect with students and staff in unique ways, they are able to recognize, praise, and encourage along the way. Even though many of our schools have a "Driver of the Month Award," they are consistently recognizing positive student and staff behavior. It's essential to reinforce the behaviors that we want to see. Administrators and teachers cannot just do this once; it must be done each time we see the behavior. This is how a culture develops a shared belief that leads to behaviors, that leads to habits, that leads to great results. So let's be consistent in recognizing what we want to see and become. If your school has the goal to be the most positive school in the district, you must identify and then point out and reinforce those behaviors. When behaviors like this are celebrated in the classroom, or through a quick conversation as well as in front of an entire school, the culture rapidly improves and transforms. Be consistent and you will see consistent impact.

Chapter 4

Fuel Your Ride with Positive Energy

"I have found that where there is a void, negativity will fill it so we must keep fueling up with positive energy, so the negativity energy doesn't have room to expand. We must fuel up daily with positive thoughts, cultivate positive feelings, and take positive actions. Positive energy is all about these things. Without it your ride will stall."

—*The Energy Bus*, page 48

One of the most effective ways to build a posi-tive school culture is to fuel every aspect of the school with positivity. In the previous chapter, we discussed the importance of consistency in creating culture. Positive schools strive to create positive environments, but it does not happen overnight. It also does not happen accidentally. One major thing that truly separates positive and driven schools from others is the ability to consistently communicate in a way that shares positive energy that fuels others.

Fueling your school with positive energy begins with the leader fueling themselves, then fueling their staff, the staff fueling the students and the entire school fueling parents, families, and the community. Positive energy cascades and spreads and transfers to others. At Keystone Elementary, one of our first model Certified Energy Bus Schools, they saw the immediate impact of this ripple effect. They committed to being one of the first Energy Bus Schools. They also committed to making the Energy Bus principles come alive on campus. The "fuel your ride with positive energy" principle impacted many on campus.

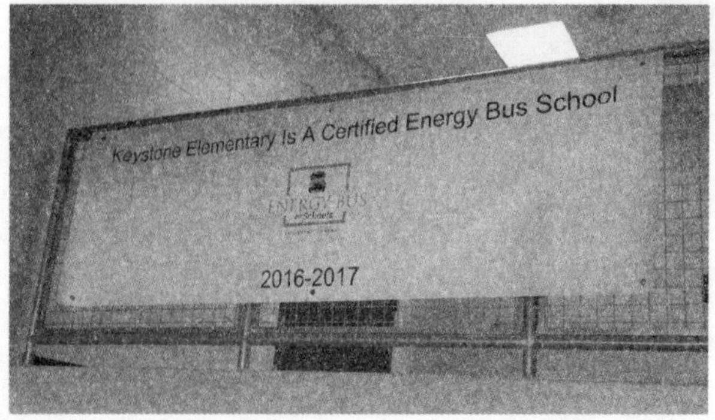

Keystone Elementary in Ohio was one of the very first Energy Bus Schools to fuel their ride with positive energy, and they felt the impact.

Fuel Yourself

It always starts with the leader. Since leadership is a transfer of belief, school leaders and teachers must focus on getting their heads and hearts in the right place. These individuals must fuel themselves up as leaders so they can fuel others.

A positive mindset is key when it comes to successful and positive leadership. Now more than ever, schools need positive leaders who are fueling themselves the right way. If you don't have positivity you can't share it. Also, if you don't have it, you can't help others who are struggling with their mindset. I (Jon) have spent much of my writing and speaking career working with school leaders and have seen firsthand the impact my books and talks have on school leaders. In fact, the Energy Bus for Schools came about because so many principals and teachers became more positive and impactful after reading it. Let's face it, being an educator is challenging and can be draining. That is why strategies and practices to develop a positive mindset are essential.

When we visit schools for workshops, we often do station work where we put all the Energy Bus principles on the walls. Participants are asked to visit each principle and complete an activity or answer a question. At the "Fuel Your Ride with Positive Energy" station, there is one simple question: How do you stay positive in a noisy, negative, and busy world?

First off, let's acknowledge it has always been a noisy and negative world, but things seem to be more negative since 2020. Self-care is often the first thing we ignore when things get busy and the days get long. We must remember that when we invest in ourselves, we are better able to invest in others.

So, how do you stay positive in a noisy and negative world. Common answers such as exercise more, eat better, read, spend time with family, go outside, and yes, even have a responsible drink. The last one always gets a laugh and is usually circled and starred by other teachers in the workshop. Many teachers and leaders simply say a nice glass of wine is a great way to unwind after a long week at school. At a school district in metro Denver, they have a dedicated building for teachers and administrators to host trainings and gain professional development. I (Jim) spoke here in 2021 and was informed the building also hosts a happy hour for teachers. I am sure this is probably one of the more popular buildings in the district.

Educators need a way to decompress, relax, and practice positive and healthy habits. Leaders are always so focused on serving others that they forget about serving themselves. How can school leaders and teachers impact others with positive energy if their cups are always empty? When taking a hard look at priorities, self-care must be at the top of the list.

I (Jon) often recommend meditation, mindfulness, prayer, or other strategies that help you lessen the clutter in your mind. As I wrote in *The One Truth*, the brain is an antenna, and we must tune into the positive each day instead of the negative.

My two favorite practices to do this I wrote about in *The Energy Bus*. The first is a Thank You Walk. This is when you walk and practice gratitude for things in your life big and small. Even 10 minutes will have a big impact. Research shows you can't be stressed and thankful at the same time. When you practice gratitude, you flood your brain and body with positive emotions that energize you instead of draining you.

The second practice is to create a success journal and each night write down your success of the day. What you focus on shows up more in your life. What you look for, you will find. Each night you will go to bed a success and wake up a success. I highly recommend you also do this with your students. My hope is that every teacher in the world will ask their students at the end of school what their success was that day. The student will go to bed every night feeling like a success.

Optimism and Belief

When you fuel your mind and brain with positivity, this helps you develop positive habits. What we believe so often determines what we create. Optimism and belief are the fuel that positive school leaders need to drive results and create the future. At George Welch Elementary, in Louisiana, Assistant Principal Anna Redding believes the everyday grind at schools is not something to overlook.

She is always looking for ways to show her staff she believes in them. Her school shares constant reminders for all who come on campus to have positive beliefs. When you enter the campus you are greeted with a huge bulletin board filled with positive affirmations and Energy Bus slogans. Ms. Redding believes it is really hard to complain about something as you walk in and out of school when you have to walk by the gigantic Energy Bus display in the front.

The best part about positivity, optimism, and belief is that it's contagious. The more you share it, the more it spreads throughout your campus.

Schools that have this kind of positive energy are just different and stand out in an amazing way. Leadership is a transfer of belief. It transfers from the leader to the staff and from the staff to the students and from the entire school to the families and the community. Positive school leaders and Energy Bus Schools have the power to transform communities and the world. It starts with you!

One of the keys to having a positive and optimistic mindset is to talk to yourself. Many of you reading this will chuckle because we all know teachers are very good at this. Teachers have told us many times in workshops how they have been caught multiple times talking to themselves out loud. We have all been there. You can also talk to yourself internally as well. We all have two dogs inside of us. One is giving us positive encouragement, speaking truth, and filling you with confidence. The other is noisy and filling your head with lies, doubt, fear, and anxiety. Who will win? The one you feed. Educators must feed the positive dog every day.

Negative thoughts often come from fear and fear often lies to us. Fear can be conquered with a positive and optimistic outlook. It does not mean we ignore fear, but we are no longer controlled by it, we overcome it. Working in schools can breed fear since there is so much unknown each day. Unknown futures breed anxiety. Unchecked anxiety will lead us to not becoming the school leader and teacher we want to be. Kasey Huebner, former principal at Spirit Lake Elementary and now the superintendent at Panorama Community Schools, believes constant conversations as a staff and reflections are required to continually fuel everyone's ride with positive energy. It's during these times of reflection that we can win the mental battle of becoming more positive and optimistic together. By staying positive and believing together, we can conquer fear and work with confidence. A staff that believes together, succeeds together.

Collective Teacher Efficacy

A few years ago, John Hattie released ground-breaking research on the new number-one influence related to student achievement. He and his team called it "collective teacher efficacy," which is the collective belief of a school staff in their ability to positively affect students. A school staff that believes it can collectively impact students is vital for the health of a school and student success. If a school staff believes it can make a difference, then it does. We often underestimate the importance of belief or think that belief and positivity is a just nice way to live, but what Hattie's research says is that belief is fundamental to creating great results. Albert Bandura, an early researcher on school culture and psychology, defines this efficacy as a group's shared belief in capabilities to accomplish a desired action or goal. Thus, you and your staff must collectively believe your students can create extraordinary outcomes. Classroom teachers must transfer this belief to their students. In turn, the students must believe that they, collectively, can find success in the classroom and build a culture of learning and respect.

A belief in creating a positive culture and fueling your ride with positive energy produces extraordinary results. These results are not always quantifiable, but you can feel them. You can feel a shift in culture and attitude with a group of people dedicated to one positive mission. The Energy Bus is so powerful because it unites the school with one mission and collective belief. At Mt. Washington Middle School, their principal, Tim Ridley, did a survey of his staff and students on the impact of the Energy Bus. He wanted an accurate look at how the Energy Bus was playing a role in helping them build their positive culture and belief. The candid responses from the students and staff showed a group dedicated to believing they can and do make a difference in the outcomes of school culture. Their collective belief was stronger than fear or doubt, and they used it to drive their bus forward.

Tim shared the survey with us and the responses were powerful. Students indicated the Energy Bus had shown them that staying positive not only can make you feel better but can impact everyone around you. Another staff member wrote that the Energy Bus has impacted the school culture by showing them how to say positive things to each other and the impact of these words. Students and staff talked about the negative impact of poor attitudes. No one wanted to be negative, and the school appreciated learning about how to deal with negativity. One of the most powerful student responses mentioned how the Energy Bus had helped them to choose better people to spend time with. As we discussed, collective belief doesn't happen by accident. It must be cultivated.

College Park Elementary did a great job of cultivating a collective, positive belief. They didn't have the space to host all-campus assemblies, but creatively, they figured out how to do it in a virtual environment. They hosted monthly assemblies led by one of their amazing counselors, Amanda Tolbert. She created an interactive and engaging environment with all the students while reinforcing the themes from *The Energy Bus* book. She often came in costume and had the students participate using microphones in their rooms. Students felt energized by her real energy and the consistency of these assemblies. The consistency is important because assemblies and trainings should not be completed when morale is low, or they need a spark. It should be done monthly and reinforced daily. Schools and districts should not wait for the tanks to be empty to invest in cultivating and maintaining their collective belief.

Fueling Staff

One of my favorite events in which I (Jim) have participated involved the Anne Arundel School District in Maryland. They hosted an innovative event called Carver at Night. This night of professional development was so popular it had a long waiting list to attend. You read that correctly: professional development that teachers were coming to in droves. They held it at a district building in the evening, and the night featured a nice meal and music from one of the local high school bands. After dinner, each participant attended sessions throughout the evening. There were also snack stations, a yoga room, a massage room, and other learning opportunities. I held a fun breakout session on the Energy Bus, where we interacted through activities and discussions. The participants were energized, encouraged, and wanted to be there.

I talked to the head of professional development, Helen Mateosky, who brought the idea to the school district. Helen found a sincere way to fuel the rides of teachers and staff with Anne Arundel Schools. It was unlike anything these staff members had been a part of, and it showed in everyone's enthusiasm and excitement. School leaders can use this example to invest in a new kind of professional development, with the freedom and ability to choose sessions for growth.

Carver at Night figured out the formula to create engagement in school culture. If you add some choice to the process and truly show all involved that you appreciate them, people will get on the bus. If they feel cared for, they will share more. They will share their positive energy with the campus and all they encounter.

There are countless ways to fuel your teachers and let them know you care about them. One of these ideas has become very popular with our Energy Bus Schools. It is a snack cart service for teachers and staff members. Some counselors and select students go around the school with a cart full of a variety of snacks. Each teacher and staff member chooses whatever they want and receives an encouraging quote or other positive words of affirmation. You can see the joy and accomplishment on the faces of the students who were able to help with this activity.

We realize not every school has the resources to create a Carver at Night event or a snack cart service. There are many ways to fuel teachers and students where the only costs are time and energy. Mt. Washington Middle School starts all their staff meetings with positive news celebrations where highlights, successes, and positive news is shared. Many schools call it something different, like "Share a Success" or "Positive Drivers Wanted," but regardless of what you call it, this practice unifies the staff, energizes them, and creates collective positivity.

Spirit Lake Elementary makes it a point to consistently show appreciation to staff members. Nancy Kriener will hand-deliver positive notes to staff members each week in the shape of a yellow school bus. Leadership teams invest time in creating new ideas on how to show appreciation to others on campus throughout the year. Spirit Lake believes these consistent ideas and engagement helps to keep school morale high. Staff feel fueled, loved, appreciated, heard, and supported.

Diplomat Elementary in Cape Coral, Florida, is a great example on how to fuel each other's rides. They not only

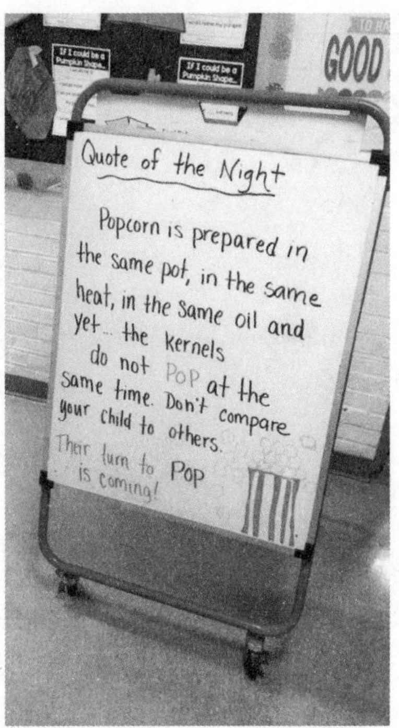

Carver at Night is an innovative approach to engaging professional development in Maryland.

retain staff members, but they have a line of applicants wanting to work there. Principal Chuck Vilardi is an example of a leader who goes to great lengths to have real relationships with all staff members. Additionally, he listens to them and always fights for the resources the school needs to be successful.

Principal Vilardi has been the leader of several schools in the Cape Coral area. One common link between his time at these schools is a commitment to building a positive

Students at Energy Bus Schools love helping with the teacher snack carts.

campus culture. Everywhere Mr. Vilardi has gone, he has used a Jon Gordon book to infuse energy and life onto his campus. His staff is highly engaged during professional development because they feel fortunate and happy to be at his campus. In an era of staff shortages, Diplomat Elementary involves staff in the school improvement process, strengthens relationships, brings in interesting and relevant professional development, and, of course, feeds the staff very well. I (Jim) have conducted workshops for three of Mr. Vilardi's schools, and they are all memorable. I remember working with enthusiastic staff members who could not imagine working anywhere else. These teachers and staff members are fully on the "Energy Bus" and they work hard to fuel each other's rides every day.

Fueling Students

As we know, it's not just the staff that needs more positivity. Students also benefit greatly from being fueled with positive energy. Keystone Elementary provided many activities and ideas that laid the groundwork for our Certified Energy Bus for Schools program. We now have a clear roadmap on how to best fuel the rides of students on campuses. The average student will spend over 10,000 hours in the elementary and secondary classroom, according to a recent article in *Education Week*. This number shows the importance of making sure every hour counts during students' education.

When you fuel a student's ride with positive energy, you are investing in their character, mindset, goals, dreams, and future. The mind, like anything else, needs to be properly trained to think positive and respond to the challenges of life. When negative events happen, the survival instinct inside of us may tempt us to hide, complain, become selfish, and disengage. This is instinctively done to protect ourselves. Students need to learn how to rise up in the face of negativity and overcome it. Schools must teach more than classroom subjects. Teaching SEL (social-emotional learning) and positive mental frameworks can be life changing.

Many of our Certified Energy Bus Schools, like Keystone Elementary, start the day with a morning meeting. In elementary schools, this is a unique opportunity to talk about what is going on in the lives of students. The key is to personalize the meeting and establish some common interests between students. This helps create positive relationships. Teachers should always end on a positive note with a class-created cheer, reciting of the school/class motto or phrase, or an Energy Bus principle. For middle and high schools, you can spend the first five minutes talking informally to build relationships since many do not meet in a homeroom.

A popular part of the Energy Bus program is the Positive Fueling Station for when a student needs a positive boost. Staff and students create notebooks with funny pictures, sayings, inspirational quotes, and photos from campus. Students can visit one of the stations and have a laugh, become inspired, and hit reset on a situation. Keystone Elementary developed this idea beyond the Energy

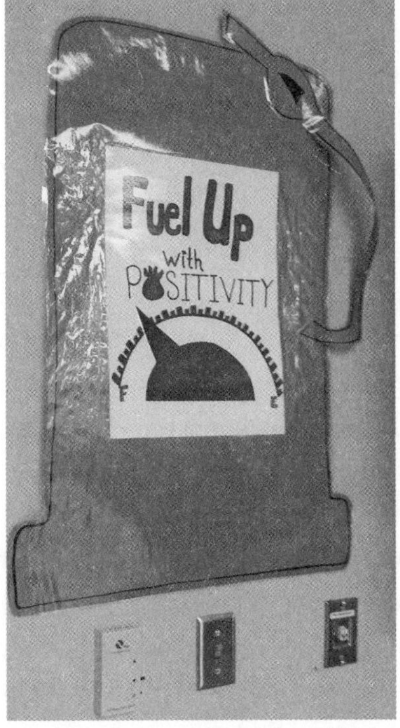

Positive Fueling Stations give staff and students a place to inspire each other.

Bus for Schools program resources. Our program has a way of inspiring the whole campus to think of innovative ideas for campus growth and how to do it.

Fueling the ride of students also means focusing on what they are doing right. The morning meeting comes into play to implement this principle. This does not mean we ignore negative behavior, but schools reinforce and encourage the positive behavior it wants to see. By sending home notes, developing awards, and praising students daily, teachers reinforce the correct behaviors. When we focus on what students are doing right, they will do more things right more often.

The Energy Bus teaches educators how to think and talk differently with students too. Teachers are encouraged to switch negative words into positive action statements. Instead of "Don't do this," try "I'd like to see you try it this way." Positive schools work to remove negative words and focus on positive words and phrasing. This shift in mindset and language teaches students to be more aware of their words as they go through the day. Energy Bus riders are encouraged to be positive, encouraging, and self-aware at school and at home too.

One teacher at Keystone Elementary said that students and faculty now feel like they have the power to own their feelings because of the Energy Bus program. Many believe they can choose to be more positive now. They feel empowered to make better choices on how they will respond inside and outside of school. Keystone teachers continually said in interviews that they feed off each other's positive energy.

Fueling the rides of students is truly a team effort. It begins with the leader. You practice self care and feed yourself. The leader then transfers that belief to the staff and fuels their ride with positive energy. The staff members in turn fuel students and parents. Together everyone wins.

Chapter 5

Love Your Passengers

"Your team wants to know that you are concerned about their future and welfare. They need to know that you love them. It can't be just about you and your job. It also has to be about them. And when you love them, they'll love you back by working hard for you, by being loyal to you, by surprising you with amazing initiative and success stories, and by teaching you as much as you will teach them."

—*The Energy Bus*, page 115

Loving is Caring

In *The Energy Bus*, I (Jon) share 5 ways to love your passengers.

1. Make time for them

2. Listen to them

3. Recognize them

4. Serve them

5. Bring out the best in them

The truth is you won't do any of these things if you don't care about people. Loving and caring are the ultimate ways you fuel your staff and students with positive energy.

Over the years, many different stories of unique and caring leaders have surfaced: the classic story of Doug Conant at Campbell's Soup writing over 10,000 thank-you notes to employees, or Indra Nooyi, the former CEO of Pepsi, writing over 400 letters each year to the parents of her senior executives. Each letter talked about what the employee was doing at the company and thanked them for the gift of their child at Pepsi. Both are bold moves that require time, organization, and commitment. Once a leader starts that process, employees—and their parents—will be on the lookout for future showings of appreciation and gratitude.

This is where the school leader or teacher can develop their caring trademark. Nooyi at Pepsi and Conant at Campbell's Soup had their own caring trademarks. Both CEOs maintained a visible presence in the lives of their employees. A visible presence will work to build trust. As we go through this section, start to think about how you uniquely care for and love your staff and students.

Drew Watkins, the former superintendent at Prosper ISD, in Texas, retired after 34 years of service and 18 years as superintendent. In his tenure, he took the time to know every student by name and personally wrote a note to every graduating senior. After starting with 80 graduates, the district rose to over 400. Many wrote that it is very clear that he loves his students, and they love him back. One student remembered him walking over to her as she was eating a peanut butter and jelly sandwich. She was a junior in high school, and he said "still don't like the crust huh?" referring to when she was in elementary school. He was actively present in his students' lives. One parent

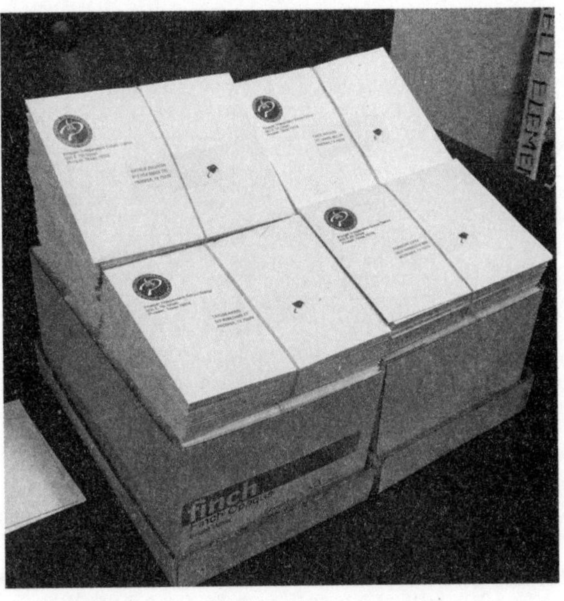

Letters written by Drew Watkins, former superintendent at Prosper ISD in Texas.

commented that her son was so excited that he got a card from the superintendent that he went over and thanked Dr. Watkins. The superintendent said students like that are the reason why he still writes all those notes. He was often seen at car lines around the district opening doors and writing notes on whiteboards in various classrooms.

He is the epitome of a relationship builder and a servant leader. Dr. Watkins developed his caring trademark as being a visible leader. Students, parents, staff, and community members felt a personal relationship with this leader of a large school district. Imagine if more school leaders and teachers took the initiative to develop and build relationships with everyone around them. Being a visible leader shows you are relationship-driven because you open yourself up to conversations and ideas. Even small stop-and-chats are great ways to show you care and love others.

One of our Energy Bus for Schools principals high-fives every elementary student who comes in the door in the morning. He says it gives him joy to see their faces, make a connection, say their name, and give that encouraging high-five.

It's essential for teachers to share their care and love as well. Susan Englert, a former gifted and English teacher at Palm Harbor Middle School, who recently retired, made it her mission to engage with students in a unique way. Her classes always felt different than others as she used project-based learning to put students in meaningful activities. There was never a moment where there was not collaboration with other students or herself. She taught with a very conversational style that drew you into the discussion. It was the kind of class you ran to and looked forward to. Every day was different, and you enjoyed the relationships around you. It felt like a family. Creating unique and engaging environments like Mrs. Englert's takes a lot of work and intentionality. However, her lessons stand the test of time, and she still keeps in touch with students from over 30 years ago.

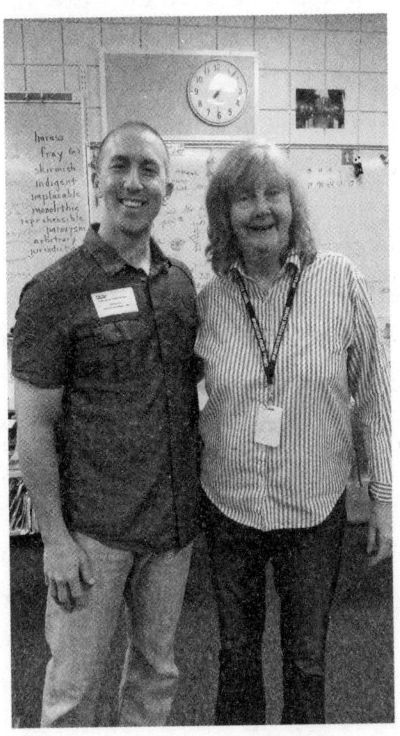

Dr Jim Van Allan with Palm Harbor Middle School gifted teacher Mrs. Susan Englert.

Building Intentional Relationships

When you love and care, you make the time to invest in and build relationships. This increases engagement and retention. According to research from the University of California-Berkeley, positive relationships among school faculty leads to a higher level of trust between each other. Additionally, coworkers see each other as accepting, encouraging, and feel they can openly communicate and ask for help when needed. Dorie Miller Elementary, in Ennis, Texas, has been a model Energy Bus School since 2017. We mentioned in Chapter 3 that they have an actual "Energy Bus" parked outside campus. It was very apparent since day one that they were all in on the Energy Bus and loving their passengers. Their long-term principal, Lindsey Wood, tells her staff she loves them often and with intention. This intentionality is behind everything Dorie Miller Elementary does for staff and students. Lindsey is intentional about making time to stop by and visit with staff or ask about their families and kids. If someone has been out sick for an extended period or is home with a new baby, she is intentional about setting alarms on her phone to check on them often. These are positive habits that lead to a passenger feeling loved, appreciated, and valued. When a school leader takes the time to reach out directly to someone who is in need, it shows that they are valued and they matter.

Showing staff love at Dorie Miller Intermediate in Texas.

The daily grind of campus life and managing staff as well as hundreds—even thousands—of students and their parents carries a lot of weight. We know it's not easy to always show you care and invest in relationships. It can be easy to let individuals get lost in the busyness of a school day throughout the year. However, when you make time for your relationships, your relationships will make your school stronger and better.

Social Glue

Intentional habits that build relationships are the social glue for a culture to develop. The University of Minnesota and University of Toronto study that looked at a link between student achievement and talented leadership gave another strategy to help build connections. They found successful principals made 20 to 60 classroom visits and observations per week. Physical presence and making time to show up and connect builds relationships and bonds of trust.

According to an article on Cleveland.com, one principal who believes in the power of social glue worked at Independence Middle School in Ohio. Kevin Jakub, now the principal of an Ohio high school, uses the strategy of a mobile office, which is a standing desk on wheels. He believes this gave him an opportunity to get out of his office. He wanted to be in the hallways, classrooms, gym, cafeteria, and anywhere staff and students are interacting and developing social bonds. Jakub said that there are so many great things happening each day within the school he wanted to be right where the action is because he believes that relationships are not built behind a desk. This gave him the opportunity to be creative with his space and where he works.

When applied consistently and with intentionality, social glue is what holds a campus together. Relationships drive nearly everything that happens on a campus and inside a classroom. Social glue is made up of individual and group conversations, intentional acts of love, visible leadership, and strategic communication that create a shared experience. There are countless ways to apply social glue with students, staff, and parents. Let's discuss some more strategies.

Loving Your Staff

The hit comedy show *The Office* showcased a little-known American holiday called National Pretzel Day, which occurs each year on April 26. In a famous scene, the boss and lead character Michael Scott stops in the middle of his workday—despite pressure from corporate about productivity—to get a free pretzel with all the fixings. Michael and his employee Stanley Hudson often had disagreements but that day they were able to bond over the joy of sharing a free pretzel.

Dorie Miller honored National Pretzel Day with free soft pretzels for all their staff. Principal Lindsey Wood works on a social calendar during summer to determine the days staff will receive hand-delivered treats. Lindsey looks at this as an opportunity to touch base with everyone one-on-one. She believes the little treats are nice, but the real way she shows her love is through intentional conversations and communication. Handwritten notes are a caring trademark of hers, and she writes at least one to each staff member every week. Lindsey tries to make the note personal to their circumstances, so they know they are loved and appreciated. This also requires her to be a present leader. She can't know what is going on in the lives of staff members without being present on campus to talk and interact with people.

Birthdays are a great way to engage with staff too. Rather than waiting until the week of their birthday to write the card—because something always comes up when you're a principal—Lindsey writes out the birthday cards in advance and has her secretary put them in the mail the week of that person's birthday. Building leaders sometimes need to get creative to ensure every staff member feels loved and special.

Dorie Miller Intermediate celebrating National Pretzel Day.

George Welch Elementary, another model Certified Energy Bus School, focuses on loving their passengers as well. Anna Redding, their assistant principal, said it is her goal to make every teacher feel valued and loved. She developed a strategy called TGIM, or "Thank Goodness It's Monday." She encourages staff and students to think about what they *get* to do today. She often puts a treat in each staff member's box and a handwritten note of encouragement or recognition. Anna believes that when she and others in leadership are positive encouragers, it will make teachers more comfortable to approach her, ask questions, and share ideas. While many focus on getting to Friday, Anna does not want anyone to have "a case of the Mondays" at George Welch Elementary.

Another creative way to recognize staff is letting the parents do it. Lindsey Wood at Dorie Miller encourages parents to send in a "Positive Staff Referral" when they want to brag on a teacher. She will print out the email and put it on a certificate, which is hand-delivered to their room. They take a picture and share it on their official school Facebook page. Lindsey made it clear that this does not cost any money, takes very little time, and has a lasting impact on teachers feeling loved, recognized, and celebrated for a job well done.

Remember, it is more than just the slip of paper. It is about the entire process and intentionality behind the system that is in place. The principal creates a system where love can flourish daily. The system allows parents and staff members to show direct appreciation for someone, and they are recognized in a public manner. While teachers don't do it for the attention or public praise, it may come at a time when they need it the most. There might be a lull in their mood or morale, and on that day it may really help them to see the positive referrals and notes from parents and students.

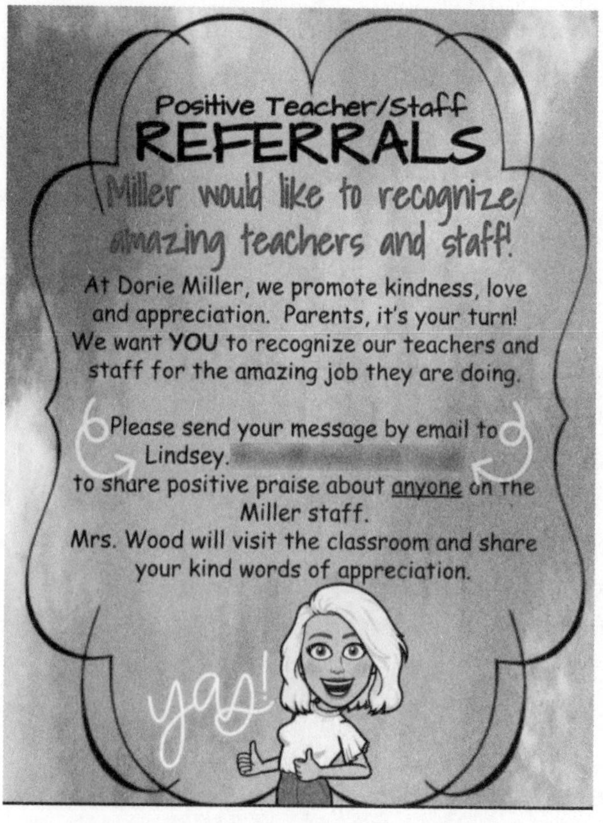

At Dorie Miller, parents are encouraged to email a "positive referral" to recognize outstanding efforts by teachers and staff.

Jessica Hanson and Amy Rollman with Azle ISD, near Fort Worth, Texas, believe fully in loving your passengers. After both of them became inspired by using the Energy Bus on their respective school campuses as principals, they wanted to pay it forward. They became certified trainers and now they are inspiring and loving on staff and teachers inside of their district. They have become the go-to people for staff development and use the principles of the Energy Bus to show others what quality leadership is like within Azle ISD. They even have the opportunity to address new faculty members and talk about these principles as the foundation for the culture within the school district. They are great examples that love grows and flourishes and helps others flourish when it is shared.

Loving Your Students and Parents

Spirit Lake Elementary brought their students to a local theme park to teach them all about the Energy Bus rules. Different stations were set up in front of theme park rides with different Energy Bus rules. Students had to learn the rule and do a fun activity before they could ride the attraction. This was a unique way to bring the Energy Bus to life for students and parents. Students are very hands-on visual learners, so Spirit Lake left a lasting impression on them with this field trip. They proved you can learn and ride rollercoasters at the same time. Spirit Lake even brought students back to the theme park as they "embarked on

Years 2 and 3" inside the Certified Energy Bus for Schools program. Their principal told us he was convinced students could thrive through adversity based on the energy he saw at the theme park. Now when students interact with the Energy Bus principles in their classrooms, they have positive feelings and impressions about them. Once

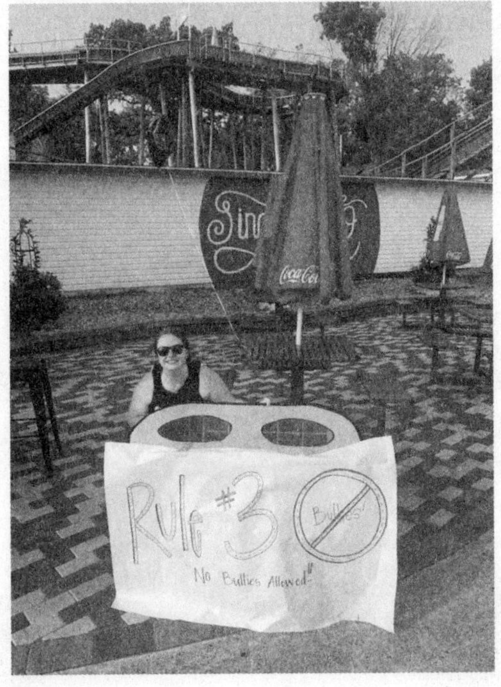

Spirit Lake Elementary takes school to a theme park to reinforce Energy Bus for Schools rules.

again this demonstrates an intentional staff and building leadership who want to love their passengers using action through an intentional process.

Spirit Lake even continued this interactive tradition with an engaging winter open house. They decorated all their hallways with different winter and Christmas themes and had the Energy Bus rules tied to each theme. This was done to showcase their various campus initiatives to parents and guests and to continue to reinforce the Energy Bus rules to everyone. Students were able to show their parents around campus and teach them the different Energy Bus rules as they walked around. They had interactive games, food, and various displays everywhere

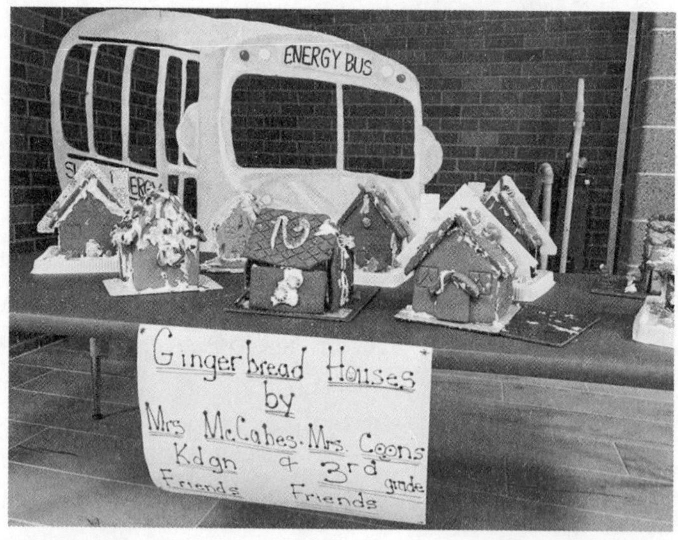

Spirit Lake showcases the Energy Bus themes with a winter open house.

you looked. Spirit Lake showcases a vibrant and energized campus community that has the Energy Bus as their foundation for everything they do.

Additionally, schools can look to practical practices to add a dose of love to the day. At Central Boulevard Elementary, they created "Fuel Your Ride Fridays" to continue the Energy Bus concept. Their school psychologist, Dr. Louis Ricci, asks staff members to read a story, a poem, or a rap over the announcements. He even uses his trombone to get some energy going around the school. It's important to use the morning announcements to set the tone for the day and reinforce culture and the Energy Bus on campus. By finding ways to creatively convey a message, students and staff will listen and remember the messaging. Who doesn't like a good rap in the morning?

One of the main questions we receive from new Energy Bus Schools is how to get the parents involved in the culture-building process so they feel the love. They know that parents are a part of their culture and must be engaged. Fortunately, with all our schools coast to coast, there are always schools sharing best practices in our monthly group coaching Zoom sessions to offer support, guidance, and examples. We are fortunate to be a large program that still has roots in making everything small, simple, and personal.

St. David Schools in Arizona were one of the first to develop an open house/dinner night for parents to introduce the concepts from the Energy Bus. They invited parents to campus for a free dinner while talking about the Energy Bus rules through presentations and skits. They found a format that works very well for their campus community, as did Spirit Lake with their strategy. The key is to bring parents on campus in some capacity. We have suggested to many of our Energy Bus Schools that they create Energy Bus rules stations around campus during an open house at the beginning of the year. Different students can run each station as they educate parents about how the Energy Bus rules are impacting everyone.

While parents coming to campus is very important, the communication at home needs to be a priority as well. Dorie Miller Elementary believes in the power of a handwritten note, so teachers are required to send home nine positive postcards every nine weeks. Principal Lindsey Wood provides the stationery for all teachers. The parents and students have given wonderful feedback about receiving these in the mail. Many parents display these notes on refrigerators, and students hang the notes on bedroom mirrors or display them in their binders.

Since the Energy Bus for Schools program is meant for all levels of schools, we are proud of the middle and high schools we have in the program as well. One of our model middle schools is Marine View in Huntington Beach, California. Principal Sarah Schaible used the Energy Bus program to energize her campus and open the lines of communication with her middle school students. Regularly throughout the school year, she would meet with Energy Bus Drivers of the Month, our award for students most engaged with the Energy Bus that month. It provided an opportunity for her, as principal, to meet with students and have small group conversations. They would talk about how the Energy Bus principles are impacting them and other issues that would arise. Sarah used those lunches as an opportunity to connect with students and build relationships. Open and transparent communication like this is a positive way to show love to students. It demonstrates that their voices and input matter in culture creation.

Marine View Middle School introduced the Energy Bus for Schools program to another middle school in their district, Vista View Middle School. Since that time, Vista View has become a model middle school for implementing the Energy Bus on campus. I (Jim) have made three separate visits to the school for a teacher workshop, student assembly, and just recently, in Fall 2023, working with their student leadership class.

Their principal, Dr. Rasheedah Gates, asked me to come back to the school to work all day with 30 of their talented student leaders. She wanted Year 2 inside of the Certified Energy Bus for Schools program to be student-driven. By giving a voice to the students, she asked that I work with them on implementing the Energy Bus principles and planning student assemblies. Ownership is the key word to describe this experience. Vista View wanted to show love to their students by giving them ownership over the school culture building process. They were able to debate, discuss, and decide how the Energy Bus program would operate on campus in the 2023–2024 school year.

Lindsey Wood, from Dorie Miller Elementary, tells her students she loves them every day via the announcements. She believes the principal sets the tone for the way kids and staff are treated on campus. Love becomes what schools do and how they do it. Lindsey always says in the announcements, "If no one told you they loved you today, Mrs. Wood is telling you that she loves you!" The schools that can find the right combination between showing and telling students they love them will see incredible results.

Dorie Miller Elementary Principal Lindsey Wood sets the tone for student encouragement.

Love and education can and should coexist. When you invite love onto a school campus, no matter the grades, you invite positivity, warmth, and intentionality. Love is the contagion you want on a campus. Love spreads through smiles, words, and actions, which encourages others to pay it forward. Deep down, we all want to be loved and appreciated, not only for the work we do but for who we are on the inside. We want to be accepted and part of the culture. No one wants to feel marginalized on a school campus. Love helps to bind and unite people together. The Energy Bus has proven to be a great vehicle to get there.

Showing Love Through Collaboration and Communication

As my (Jon's) kids were growing up, we held a weekly family meeting that united us together. Now, you can find Jim's family trying to engage in conversation with their young children. Since they were infants, Jim and his wife made it a point to eat dinner together every night they were home, without television or technology. Even at restaurants, they have a no-tablet policy. Communication is a central component of the household because that is how you truly deepen relationships. Active and ongoing communication with those around you will build up the trust required to have a strong relationship.

Communication is the foundation upon which great relationships are built and great relationships help build

Dr. Jim Van Allan holding an in-person coaching session with school leaders at Franz Elementary in Texas.

great cultures. When you add collaboration to your communication, you supercharge your relationships and culture. Successful schools are truly collaborative. We show love by having a collaborative culture because everyone is included in the shared experience. Positive campus cultures are not built with power structures and people working alone. Our Energy Bus Schools have demonstrated the blueprint, and each one of our school leaders values good communication to share their vision of excellence and work together to achieve it.

Intentional Listening

A key aspect of loving your passengers and collaboration is listening. The communication textbook *Skilled Interpersonal Interaction* suggests employees should spend 55% of their day listening, and managers should spend 63% of their day listening. The skill of listening is often an overlooked part of the communication and culture-building process. This is how we learn new information and meet the needs of others around us. This can help leaders, teachers, and students give support where it is needed. Listening is a mental process, while hearing is a physical process. We can be hearing something but not listening. For example, you can hear noise and voices around you at parties and events but not listen to them. Listening involves the brain attending to the incoming noise stimuli and doing something with that information. You will either file it away for future use or use it immediately. The best way to listen in a conversation is to paraphrase the other person as they speak, ask open-ended questions, and make mental notes about what is being said. You can also give nonverbal feedback through nods, leaning in, and facial expressions to communicate your interest. Make sure these are genuine, because people can smell fake a mile away.

We listen to show interest, gain information, and connect better with those around us. A powerful activity we do in our Energy Bus workshops is called SOLER, which stands for Seated, Open, Lean, Eyes, and Relax. Participants partner up with someone else and are told to decide who is A and who is B. The A person tells a meaningful and emotional story from their life. The B person is supposed to violate each letter deliberately yet slowly from SOLER. During the activity, you will often see people start to stand up, look at their phones, yawn, look away, and lean backwards in the middle of the story. It's all a game, of course. We then debrief the activity. People say even though they knew the activity, they still felt unimportant, sad, angry, and other wide ranges of emotion. We then give them another minute to finish the story, but this time, their partner must practice good SOLER. The mood immediately shifts around the room. The main lesson is the importance of connecting on a deeper level with the people around you. Listening and good communication are the keys to showing others you care about and love them.

Nonverbal Communication

Intentional listening is a first step, followed by a keen awareness of nonverbal communication. Nearly every communication textbook and scholar will tell you that communication is 60 to 90% nonverbal. This means that what is not said matters more than what is said. Nonverbal communication is anything except the literal content and words a person says. It is facial expressions, the way we sound, how we walk, the way we arrange a room, how we see time, body language, hand gestures, and more. It involves a person reading between the lines and not focusing solely on the obvious, which are a person's words.

In his book on body language in the classroom, Patrick Miller says a good teacher is also a good listener. It's not only about the words spoken, but also the silent messages that signal agreement/disagreement, attention/

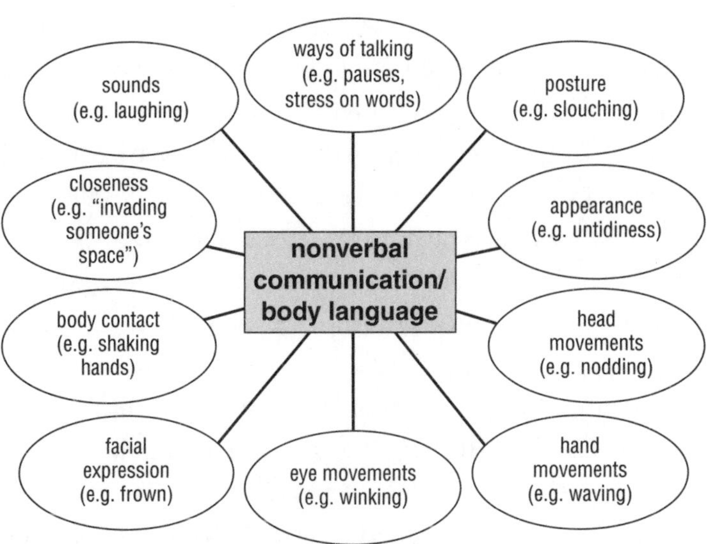

Understanding nonverbal communication is a key element for educators to become good listeners.

inattention, interest/boredom, and the desire of the student to be heard. Reading and deciphering nonverbals comes with experience but can lead to a wealth of information about people. You can truly see and understand what is happening on the inside of a person. This will allow a stronger connection because people just want to be understood. Not all feelings are obvious, but usually the nonverbals give us a glimpse into what they are thinking.

Teachers can and do use this in the classroom, and leaders should use this with faculty in meetings and one-on-ones. Take the time to sharpen your connection skills and realize that we can show love to others this way. When someone feels understood and truly heard, they feel loved. This will lead to more opportunities to strengthen that relationship on many different levels. Think about this in terms of dealing with negativity on campus as well. Difficult students or staff members may have more going on inside than meets the eye. People are not born negative and don't wake up saying "How can I ruin someone's day today?" There is usually a past trauma or hurt causing some internal strife that manifests through negativity, complaining, acting out, and lack of care or apathy toward others or initiatives. We'll discuss this in more depth in the next chapter. For now, we can use nonverbal communication to recognize there is something going on with a teacher or student, and we need to run toward them to help and not run away.

Strategic and Meaningful Interactions

We must value and include everyone on the campus and make them feel loved. We do an activity in our Energy Bus and Power of Positive Leadership trainings called Paper Mingle. Each participant is given a card with a question on it. The goal is to walk around and ask your question to as many people as you can in a partner setting, and the other person asks their question back. After responses are exchanged, you find someone else. This is one of the best parts of the training because it gets people up, moving, talking, and interacting. We always ask participants what they learned from others or what responses stood out. People love to share what they learned. We tell them to store that information and use it when they see that person again.

At the beginning of the activity, we have the audience look around, and ask how many people in the room have never spoken to someone else in here for whatever reason. Shockingly enough, even on small campuses, many hands go up, sometimes half the room. Educators are not talking to others as much as they should. Some may head in the back door and go straight for the classroom before retreating at the end of the day. While this is a completely normal strategy sometimes, it should not be the norm. I (Jim) had someone tell me from a training that they have walked by and said hello to the same person for years but never actually talked to them. Through the Paper Mingle activity, they discovered how much they have in common. Welcome to a new relationship. When you practice good communication, it leads to greater connection, love, and collaboration.

The One-on-One Interaction

It's great to love your passengers collectively but one-on-one connections are key for long-term growth and strength. Relationships take time and you are not meant to be friends with everyone on campus. However, making some effort to talk to various people outside the office, classroom or grade level shows a collaborative culture coming together.

Steven Rogelberg in the *Harvard Business Review* wrote about the value of the one-on-one for managers. His research looked at one-on-one connections not simply as an add-on to their role, but as a foundational component to it. These types of meetings can make their teams' day-to-day output better and more efficient, building trust and psychological safety. They can also improve employees' experiences, motivations, and engagement. Rogelberg conducted three studies using a global survey of 1,000 workers, a US survey of 250 people who lead or participate in one-on-ones, and interviews with 50 top leaders at Fortune 100 companies. The research supports one-on-ones for use in organizational culture if clear expectations for that meeting exist. These meetings should be focused on the needs, concerns, and hopes of the employee. The manager needs to ensure that the meetings occur, actively facilitate them, encourage genuine conversation, ask good questions, and offer support. The key is to be a facilitator and let the employee talk through the session. This is where great and intentional listening comes into play, with paraphrasing and asking questions back. Listen to understand.

No matter the size of a staff on campus, leaders can work to schedule one-on-ones and be intentional about them. We recommend connecting with one to three staff members a day for up to 10 minutes. Doing this daily over time will build great relationships and a great culture. We also recommend teachers do this with students. The research is clear. Student performance goes up when

A well-connected and loving staff at Sageland Microsociety Elementary in Texas.

they have a relationship with their teacher. Also, teacher satisfaction goes up when they have a relationship with their principal.

As Lindsey Wood at Dorie Miller Elementary told us, "frequent and intentional communication is the driving factor in creating a culture where students and staff feel loved." A job in education can be very difficult and is often thankless. Teachers and administrators pour into the lives of students every day. It is important for teachers and staff to know that building leaders see them, appreciate them, and love them for what they do. A serious investment into creating a collaborative culture full of communication and love is one of the best decisions a school leader can make.

Chapter 6

Transform Negativity

"Listen, George, you are too close to the problem to see it. The problem is that you are taking it too personally. Step back for a moment. Don't focus on these people personally. Forget they even have names. Don't think of it as you versus them. Just realize that they represent the negativity that will always be around you. The important thing is to know how to deal with the negativity and what to do with it."

—*The Energy Bus*, page 69

Negativity exists in our schools. It's a reality we can't ignore. Even the most successful schools will still have pockets of negativity. Even within our Certified Energy Bus for Schools program, principals ask us how to handle negativity that still exists. We are always coaching our schools to offer solutions and resources.

If negativity is left unchecked, it can sabotage everything leaders and their school have worked toward. Unfortunately, it seems there is more negativity than ever. The

Covid pandemic created an aftershock of stress, anxiety, and burnout. In a June 2022 Gallup poll, K–12 teachers reported the highest burnout rate of all US professions. More than 4 out of every 10 teachers noted they feel burned out "always" or "very often" at work. These teachers listed safety concerns, low salaries, funding deficits, and declining mental health as some of the main sources of stress. Requests for our school trainings, workshops, and the Energy Bus program have significantly increased since 2021. Schools feel the weight of negativity and want to invest in transforming it.

Teachers are not the only ones feeling burned out. A study published by the Yale University Center for Emotional Intelligence in early 2020 found that after surveying 21,678 US high school students, 75% self-reported negative feelings related to school. The researchers concluded that students are feeling tired, stressed, and bored. Post pandemic, countless school leaders have shared with us their desire to help students manage their mental and emotional health. Although there is not an easy solution to transforming negativity on campus, our goal is to identify some of the sources and solutions schools can utilize.

The Energy Bus Transforms Negativity

Ever since *The Energy Bus* book came out in 2007, schools have been drawn to it because it helps schools fuel up with positivity and remove negativity. This is a large reason

95

Transform Negativity

Schools embrace the Energy Bus for Schools program as part of their process of transformation.

why we created the Energy Bus for Schools program. We wanted to give schools more tools and resources to accomplish their goals.

Our speakers and trainers have spent years talking and consulting with principals across the country, and sometimes internationally, about transforming school culture. Many fill out a program or speaking request form. In the section of the form asking for "other comments/message," people in education give us all the details about what's really going on in their schools. Frequent comments include "need a spark," "low morale on campus," "tired of the negativity," "have to get everyone on track," "need positive thinking strategies for everyone." After a short phone call, it is obvious that our schools are dealing with tremendous challenges and negativity.

School leaders and teachers who really care about the future and direction of their school reach out because they want to transform negativity inside their school. Many of these educators have found *The Energy Bus* in their search for a book or thought-leader that will address exactly what they are feeling or going through. "It's life changing," as one of our Energy Bus for Schools principals shared. The book addresses the negativity that exists at work and in life. Once you read the book, it becomes clear that the main character, George, can represent a lot of different people and situations at a school. George went through a transformation, and schools can as well.

Energy Vampires

In the classic start to *The Energy Bus* book, the main character, George, wakes up one morning, goes out to his car, and notices a flat tire. His wife had warned him to fix the tire so this wouldn't happen, and as many people realize, his wife was right. Misfortune seems to follow George everywhere, and he carries around a negative attitude all the time. He feels alone and is on the verge of losing it all, including his family, because of negativity.

Negativity in schools is real and exists in many forms. The most obvious and impactful is the behavior of a negative colleague. Some come to school each day with a bad attitude and contagious negative energy. Worn down by the job, the pressure, negative parents, the system, or by the lack of support, their default mindset has become negative. Some are exhausted by hardships and challenges in their personal lives they have not dealt with. As a result, they become energy vampires who suck the life and energy out of others and the school.

I (Jim) spoke at a school where the principal pulled me aside before the session to tell me that a few teachers at the school were literally going from classroom to classroom in order to complain and gossip. She knew this was demoralizing and wanted to create a culture to eliminate that behavior.

Whatever the issues behind people's negative behavior, they are a big reason why our schools crave positive professional development. Many serious concerns are contributing factors, including teacher pay, class size, curriculum, and lack of parent support. However, if we respond to negativity with negativity, there is no growth. Many of those external factors are beyond our control. What we can control is our attitude and actions. I (Jon) taught in a school when I was getting my masters in teaching. It was my first time teaching, and I was with a group of teachers that complained constantly. At the time I remember thinking, if this is teaching, I want no part of it. Years later that experience has been a driving force to remove negativity from schools and it's why I am so passionate about this work.

It Starts at the Cultural Level

Removing negativity begins with your culture and discussing the costs and harmful impact of negativity. We recommend the school leader discuss removing and transforming negativity in the beginning of the school year and then reinforcing the message at meetings throughout the year. One school leader told her staff it was not okay to share your negativity with each other and your students because it sabotages our mission to impact students' lives. We can't let negativity ruin our mission.

Transforming Our Students

Schools must overcome negativity as a staff to help students transform their negativity. As mentioned previously, 75% of high school students self-reported negative feelings related to their school. Students are feeling tired, stressed, and bored. This study revealed that the way students feel at school affects their academic performance and their overall health and well-being. As educators, we can influence students' beliefs and mindsets in a positive way.

A new high school in the Energy Bus for Schools program in Georgia believed their students needed to learn more about personal responsibility, treating each other better, and having better control over their emotions. A large fight had broken out two days before our professional development session. One brave teacher, who had helped deescalate the situation, came into the staff workshop with her wrist in a brace. Teachers said the students needed better outlets for their thoughts and negativity. They wanted to bring in the Energy Bus for Schools program to be a stable and consistent presence of positivity on a campus that needed it. While most in the session agreed that better mental health counseling and intervention was needed, sometimes funding and staff shortages do not allow these needs to be met. This high school wanted the Energy Bus to refocus students and staff on positive thinking and positive behaviors.

One way to accomplish this is through a practice the principal started after they became a Certified Energy Bus School. After finding inspiration from the program and authors like Gerry Brooks, the principal decided to create compliment notebooks for his campus.

One person writes a compliment to another staff member in the notebook and puts it in that person's mailbox. The person who receives the compliment and notebook is to repeat the process for another staff member. As of press, the principal said there are four compliment notebooks floating around campus. One of these notebooks even gets sent to the district office to spread kindness there.

The principal told me they want to live and practice the themes from the program and book every day. If their

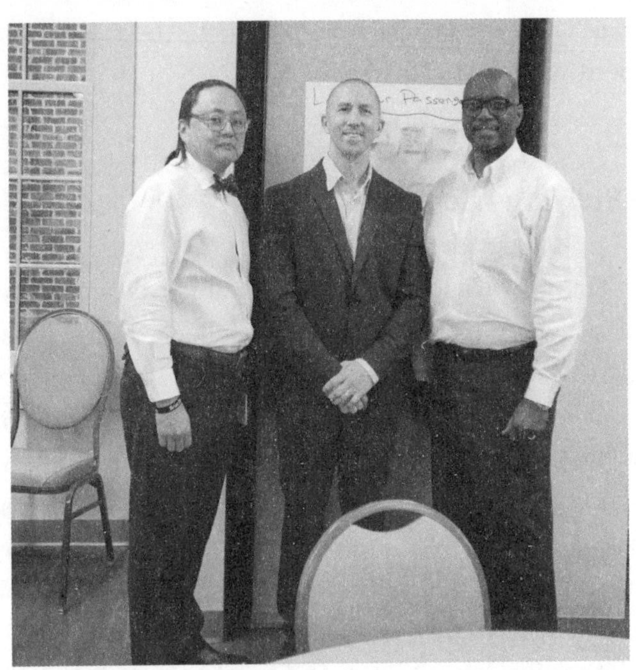

Dr. Jim Van Allan with school principals in Richmond County in Georgia.

goal is to create a positive campus culture and live it, they need to actively look for ways to do this. The compliment notebook has been a huge help in uniting staff and helping everyone to feel valued.

California-based middle schools, like Marine View and Vista View, both Energy Bus Schools, continually try to include their students in the conversation about school culture. This allows leadership to take the pulse of the school. They can tweak their initiatives, even the Energy Bus program, to address the ever-changing landscape of a school.

Things change week to week, and the best schools are responsive to these changes.

No Bullying Allowed

The Energy Bus for Schools program makes it a point to directly address negativity and bullying in the lives of students. StopBullying.gov reports that 20% of students nationwide ages 12–18 experience some form of bullying. The two most prevalent types of bullying are subjecting the victims to rumors or lies, and to insults. With the rise of social media, 15% of those experiencing bullying say it happens online. This has prompted every state in the country to enact anti-bullying legislation.

Protecting our children is one of the most important things we can do as educators and parents. It's a mission that keeps parents up at night. Parents should be able to feel comfortable sending their children to a school. If children don't feel safe, they can't learn. The Energy Bus program recognizes this need and builds in anti-bullying discussions and activities into the material.

Students have open and honest discussions in the classrooms, with each other, and at home about bullying, negativity, how it feels, and what they can do about it. Our elementary schools do a great job putting up "No Bullying Allowed" posters and teaching students to avoid bullies, to walk away, and to tell someone. We do not want our

Posters help draw attention to the idea that the school is there to help protect them from issues like bullying.

students suffering in silence. They should feel like they are part of a culture that will put their needs first, a place where they feel safe and have genuine connections with their teachers and administrators. They need to know that if they approach an adult with an issue related to negativity and bullying, someone will help them.

Unmet Needs

Mental health continues to be a priority in our country. Schools are now focusing more than ever on social-emotional initiatives, and funding is becoming more readily available. According to the American School Counselor Association, students' unmet mental health needs pose barriers to learning and development. We are seeing schools becoming more proactive in helping students and staff who have mental health issues. The Kaiser Family Foundation reported that in 2022, 96% of public schools reported offering at least one type of mental health service to their students. However, only half of those schools feel like they can offer these services effectively and consistently. There is still work to do inside our schools to help staff and students with mental health. The Energy Bus for Schools provides helpful tools.

Many issues stem from unmet needs. People are either unwilling to deal with these needs or do not realize the need is not being met. Either way can cause negativity and frustration to be expressed in unhealthy ways. Energy vampires exist because something is driving them to be negative. They may never have had positive examples around them. We tend to become our environment or what we have experienced. A campus in tune with its staff and students will recognize unmet needs and work to put a plan in place to address them.

During speaking engagements for the Energy Bus, we talk a lot about unmet needs and their ability to cause negativity. Participants analyze their feelings toward the five needs discussed next (attachment, acceptance, positive regard, autonomy, and competence) and rank them based on what they desire the most. It's important they see what might be causing distress or anxiety in their own lives.

Attachment

Most people long for some type of secure connection. We want to feel connected mentally and physically to our jobs, to people, and to our community. When we are connected, we feel secure and safe. Children experience this with the love and security of having a loving parent around when they are little. Adults need safe relationships too—at work—and when they don't find them, it leads to discouragement, division, and emptiness.

Acceptance

One of the strongest human needs is to feel accepted by those around you. This does not mean universal acceptance, where we still get accepted even if we make bad choices. It means accepting us for who we are and what we believe. It is something driving our country to unhealthy levels of division because large groups of people on all sides do not feel accepted, heard, or validated. This is leading to anger, frustration, and separation.

Positive Regard

We genuinely want to be liked and admired by others. This is positive regard. In her famous 1985 Oscars acceptance speech, Sally Field exclaimed, "I can't deny the fact that you like me. Right now, you really like me!" Sally Field led an unorthodox career, as she would put it. Between roles in the early 1960s, she struggled to be accepted and invited to auditions until her first Oscar win in 1980. This second win really convinced her that Hollywood held her in a positive light. Positive regard makes us want people to like us.

Autonomy

Even though schools are a community of diverse learners and individuals who are working toward one unified vision, we still want control over our individual lives. We want to be able to author our own decisions, manage our classrooms, and not feel overly controlled. Too much control will lead to rebellion, so letting people be themselves and having ownership of their role and responsibilities will lead to more engagement and a stronger team. Students and staff need to make the choice on their own to be part of the school culture and positive development.

Competence

Another major human need is knowing we are good at what we do. It's important that we know, and others know, that we are good at our jobs and at being a husband, wife, brother, sister, friend, and so on. Humans, especially Americans, place a high degree of value on jobs, productivity, and accomplishments. One of the first things people will ask when they meet someone is "What do you do?" This will no doubt lead to many questions and often mutual respect and admiration for each other's professions. It is no surprise that each time I (Jim) do this unmet-need activity with various educator audiences across the country, competence is the need educators most desire. The second one is always autonomy.

We jokingly say that most teachers want to be told they are good at their jobs and then be left alone! But the truth is we need to meet all our needs, and when we do we will have less negativity in a school. With that said, negativity will always persist and exist because we are not perfect, and negativity is always part of our journey and story. Every school will have to overcome negativity to define itself and create the future. Negativity will have to be addressed.

Addressing the Negativity

When addressing negativity, it is easier when the foundation is in place. Central Boulevard Elementary in Bethpage, New York, is consistently one of our model Energy Bus Schools. Their assistant principal, Julianne Inghilterra, mentioned that a positive foundation will help to transform negativity on campus. Since autonomy is a major human need, she mentions how her administration team knows individuals need to be heard and know their opinions matter. They have a culture that addresses negativity and does not let it build up.

Central Boulevard Elementary on Long Island, New York, doing an engaging assembly for students.

The following are strategies our model schools use to address negativity.

Bring Energy Vampires into the Light

As mentioned earlier, many negative people have experienced a lot of negativity in their life. Maybe their parents were poor communicators. Maybe a spouse or significant other complains a lot and is very critical. It's important they are coached though the process. A strong foundation built on relationships will show people that feedback is meant to help others grow and be better people. Energy vampires need to be brought into the light and shown the way. Negativity always wants to live in the shadows, in the corners, and behind people's backs. When we bring it into the light, we address it, manage it, and move on.

Schools must address negativity, bring energy vampires into the light, and never lose hope in their vision. South Conway Elementary knows they must deal with negativity as it arises. They intercede with people having a tough time to try to offer as much support and encouragement as possible and to resolve any issues. They establish norms with all groups of employees about how they will work together. Their expectations help them to know negativity will be brought into the light, it will be dealt with, and this will help the school to manage conflict in the future. Schools cannot hide from dealing openly and honestly with negativity.

Retrain How We Think and Process

It's not just the negative people who need to be coached through the transformation process. As we mentioned earlier, it starts at the cultural level and school leaders need to communicate the expectations for dealing with negativity with everyone. Educators must train their brains on how they deal with other people and manage their own thoughts and emotions.

Heather DeBoer, at Roosevelt Elementary in South Dakota, does a great job pouring into the lives of her staff. They focus on setting clear expectations and having plans in place that deal with negativity. Their foundation is based on positivity and relationships. She believes it is important not to allow blame to be placed on anyone when difficult conversations need to happen. Conversations like these should not be feared or looked at punitively. This is where school leaders can coach staff on the process of being more positive and dealing with negativity. To help schools cultivate positivity we teach strategies to have a more positive mindset in our workshops and also how to remove negativity.

Desert View Middle and High School, in Arizona, works to transform negativity every day on campus. They were already a great school, but wanted to become even better. According to Assistant Principal Jayleen Hackman, sending out weekly positive-thoughts emails encourages the staff and lets them know that school leadership appreciates them. They feed the positive and this helps them weed the negative.

Difficult Conversations

Coaching is an ongoing process. Sports teams offer coaching preseason, midseason, and off-season. A good coach looks for multiple ways to impact the lives of their team members. Coaches want well-rounded athletes on their team. School leaders want well-rounded educators on their school team. This means having coaching conversations when they need to happen. This often means having difficult conversations.

Everyone deals with conflict and challenging conversations differently. These conversations include serious behavior conversations, general feedback on teaching, attitude or low-morale discussions, or any conversation that may cause discomfort. Not every conversation on a school campus can be complimentary. We need to have constructive dialogue and transparent communication in order to improve.

During many of my on-campus speaking engagements, I (Jim) ask people to stand up during the section on managing negativity and conflict management. I stand on a chair in the middle of the room and hold up a sign that says "Conflict." I ask everyone to move closer or farther away depending on their level of comfort with having a difficult conversation. Like a spiderweb, people move to all corners of the room. Some people stand right near me, showing difficult conversations do not faze them, and others stand far away. One teacher even left the room and went to her car in the parking lot. Another teacher once crawled onto a library cart and wheeled herself to a corner. Others have hidden behind drapes or stood back to back with me. I always remind people to look around and see where their colleagues and administrators are standing. It helps them to understand why they sometimes act as they do. It's one of our favorite and most eye-opening activities to do with a staff. To help make difficult conversations less difficult, we suggest school leaders foster staff conversations where they deal with the elephants in the building and agree to manage emotional energy while discussing these issues. The best way to get better at having difficult conversations is to have them and grow from them. The Star 3 model, created by Jon Gordon and Amy P. Kelly, is very helpful.

STAR^3 Model

S Small ego. Big mission. We>Me.

T Truth. Tell the truth in love to get better together.

A Assume positive intent. Do not take it personally. Manage the emotional energy. No personal attacks.

R1 Remember what matters most, relationships.

R2 Respect your team and the process. Truth told in love develops respect, and respect values truth.

R3 Rules of engagement. Create specific rules of engagement for your team to have the difficult conversations in a positive way.

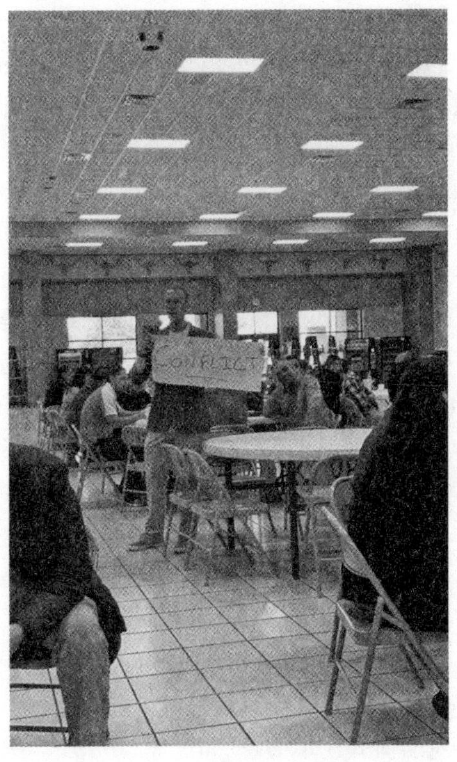

Asking people to move closer or farther away from the "Conflict" sign helps dramatize their comfort level with having a difficult conversation.

The No Complaining Rule

After the success of *The Energy Bus,* the next book I (Jon) wrote was *The No Complaining Rule,* another concept that has made a lasting impact on many organizations, including school districts seeking to transform negativity.

Dwight Cooper, the co-founder of a nursing staff agency, built one of the fastest-growing companies in the country. *Inc.* magazine gave them the distinction of being one of the best companies to work for in the country. Dwight said a big part of their success was creating a policy that eliminated mindless complaining. He called it the "no complaining rule" because even subtle complaining can ruin a culture. His company's policy is simple: you are not allowed to complain unless you also offer one or two possible solutions. These complaints must go to the right person who can do something about it.

Dwight eliminated the mindless, subtle complaining but not all complaining. Every complaint offers an opportunity to turn a negative into a positive. Some complaints can become catalysts for innovation and new processes. I am sure everyone reading this book is glad someone complained about outhouses and developed indoor plumbing.

Schools have loved the no complaining rule because it puts complaining and negativity at the forefront and proclaims that negativity will not have a place on their campus. Many schools over the years have read *The No*

Complaining Rule and instituted a policy like this on campus. This shows a willingness, effort, and plan to address mindless complaining while using justified complaints to create solutions and innovations.

It's Just Too Positive Here

Everyone in the school must have the singular, collective goal of a positive campus culture. This will lead to becoming a destination location—a place that attracts the best teachers who want to work there and parents who want to be engaged in the school that is at the center of the community. Destination locations are positive and warm places where everyone feels valued, heard, and understood.

A new principal set out to create this type of school. After having everyone read *The Energy Bus* at the beginning of the year and working the principles into conversations, meetings, and announcements everyone was determined to make it a positive place.

Well, we should say almost everyone because there was one teacher who told the principal "I've been here before you, I'll be here after you and I'm not changing." In other words, she wasn't going to change and become positive. She was going to stay negative.

The principal called us and asked what she should do. Besides documentation, we said keep building your culture so strong and get all of the staff who were not energized, but also not negative, on the bus with you. This teacher will get off the bus herself because she won't fit in. The principal went to work.

Every interaction was rooted in purpose and positivity, and a heavy emphasis was placed on staff development, teamwork, and relationships. They used the concepts from *The Energy Bus* all year. At the end of the school year, the negative teacher approached the principal and said, "I just can't work here anymore because this place is too positive!" She ended up letting herself off the bus. The following year, morale and performance soared!

Getting the right people on your bus is essential. When you need to let someone go or they let themselves off the

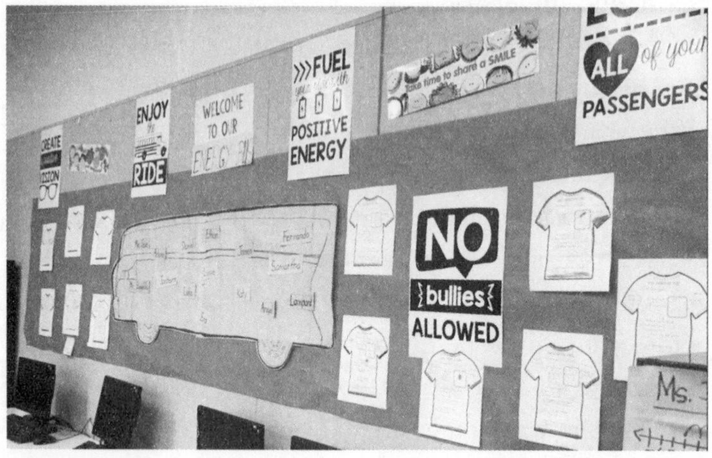

Decorations provide a visual reminder of Energy Bus rules all over campus.

bus, you allow it for the greater good. One person can break a team, and we cannot allow anyone's persistent negativity to crash our bus. So never be afraid to create a campus culture that is just "too positive to be here." Real positivity and getting rid of negativity will always make your school better.

Chapter 7

Refuel, Reenergize, and Refocus with Purpose

"Purpose is the ultimate fuel for our journey through life. When we drive with purpose we don't get tired or bored and our engines don't burn out. . . . Remember, you're driving the bus. You have the best view and vision, so you'll also need to communicate your vision and purpose with your passengers."

—*The Energy Bus*, page 131

Once there is a plan and mindset in place to transform and manage negativity on campus, schools also need to refocus on purpose. The unique challenges of a school day can compound over time. If mindsets are not focused and reenergized, our tanks may fall on empty. Despite our best efforts to remove negativity, there will be times that stress and burnout surface. It's during these times we need to refuel, reenergize, and refocus with purpose.

Central Boulevard Elementary, in Bethpage, New York, strives to continually help teachers refocus on purpose.

They teach everyone to lead with purpose and every interaction with other students and faculty on campus matter and can either energize someone or bring them down. Some teachers at the school view their purpose as being energizers. In addition to teaching, they want to lift the spirits of those around them with various displays of love and care. Central Boulevard knows that change can lead to discomfort, but they preach that it is okay to be comfortable being uncomfortable. This will lead to positive growth. Shifting mindsets away from negativity and anxiety and more toward purpose and growth will be uncomfortable at times. This is where a positive school culture and positive mindsets make a huge difference.

There Will Be Days

We understand the challenges of the modern school day on multiple levels. Previously, we looked at sources of negativity and challenges on campus. Like many of you on social media, we follow several humor and parody accounts. Sometimes it is fun to be entertained by the creative content out there, especially in the fields in which you work. When it comes to teachers and education-driven content, there is no shortage of accounts. We came across a video on social media that started out with the ABBA song "S.O.S." and the lyrics "It used to be so nice . . . it used to be so good," showing happy scenes from classic movies. Then the words "Teachers walking into 2019" flashed on the screen, with scenes like Dorothy skipping down the yellow brick road or John Travolta happily strutting down the street in *Saturday Night Fever*. Suddenly the video cut to the words "Teachers walking into 2020, 2021, then 2022 and then 2023" with the lyrics "so when you're near me, darling can't you hear me, S.O.S." Much less happy movie scenes flashed on the screen from *Alien, The Wolf of Wall Street, Rocky, The Joker,* and *Bridesmaids*. Most of the actors in the latter movies were in peril or extremely worn-out looking, walking or running from something. It was good for a laugh and a few shares.

Some of the comments said the video hit the nail on the head. There were a lot of bull's-eye and thumbs-up emojis. There is a lot of talk now about the pre-Covid "glory days" and "It didn't used to be like this." Educators need to be shown grace because we believe they have the most challenging but meaningful, impactful job on the planet. There will be many days that they see their students smile, or learn something for the first time and say "wow" or finally get the teaching and the light bulb in their mind goes on. There will be days it's all worth it. There will be those days, though, that make you want to give up.

There will be days when you simply don't feel like coming to school. There will be days when you have more challenges than you are prepared for. There will be days when a school administrator does not feel like walking the halls, smiling, shaking hands, and making conversation. Parents may call or email asking the same questions repeatedly, even though the school had sent five different forms of communication. There will be days when you forget to eat, drink water, or even smile for part of the day. There will be days when you need to put on a movie or video so you can catch your breath, and there's nothing wrong with that. There will be days when there seems to be one mini-crisis after another, and you are not sure how you can rebound from this. There will be days when students talk a lot, don't listen, and probably reflect some of the parenting at home. We cannot control what happens at home, even though we wish we could. There will be days when being positive is not the easiest or most natural thing to do. This is where we must tap into our own bigger purpose. After all, there is no greater purpose than being an educator and impacting our students' lives and helping them create their future.

The ING Foundation revealed that 88% of people say a teacher had a significant and positive impact on their life. The same study suggests 83% of those surveyed said they had a teacher who helped build their confidence and self-esteem. Every person in education will have "those days" but our purpose will reenergize and refocus us. So let us remind you that you are here for a purpose and you do make a difference!

Planting the Seed

Celebrities, athletes, actors and actresses, musicians, and influencers may get a lot of the glory for helping others with charity work; however, you don't have to be famous to make an impact. You just have to serve others with purpose, and in turn you will have a massive influence on others—a genuine influence where people will remember your impact as your legacy. As educators, let your purpose be rooted in the amazing impact you have on a generation of learners who need you in their lives. They may not remember every lesson or concept, but they will remember the experience and support you provided them at a very important time in their lives.

We don't get burned out because of what we do; we get burned out because we forget why we do it. As educators it's essential to remember your why. Why you do what you do. Each day plant yourself like a seed where you are focused on making a difference and you will grow into the life changer you are meant to be. The research is clear that when people are using their strengths and gifts for a bigger purpose beyond themselves, it can energize them. So on the days you don't feel positive, remember your purpose and it will give you something to be positive about.

Schools on a Mission Know Their Purpose

Great schools and school leaders constantly and consistently talk about their purpose and what they stand for. They ensure that everyone connected to campus knows their purpose of why they come to school each day and why they entered the education profession in the first place. Desert View Middle and High School in Arizona have a mission to educate with knowledge, empower with character, and equip students for life. They told us they want their students to be decent human beings. Character building and showing kindness are core values at Desert View. This mission led them to become Certified Energy Bus Schools because our principles aligned with their mission. Desert View knows what they stand for and reinforces with faculty and staff how their purpose and school mission are linked together.

Some schools are just beginning to understand what they stand for. Many schools decide "positivity" or "unity" will be what they stand for, so they bring in *The Energy Bus* book and program to guide them. One high school in the Triumph Public High Schools group in Texas uses *The Energy Bus* to create strong bonds between staff members, which gives them a better identity. They know what they want to stand for and that is refocusing back to culture. They had done book studies in the past, but none were as successful or impactful as *The Energy Bus*. The principal told us it was the first time ever they had almost every staff member take a book, actually read it, and make notes in the book. Each staff member brought their copies of the book to their first staff meeting with highlights and sticky notes hanging from all the pages. The principal knew they were headed down the right road.

South Conway Elementary is a school that is also rooted in purpose. Their principal, Leon Hayes, told us he believes that purpose is all about why we do what we do, and that education is a calling. He also knows his purpose and mission and reinforces this concept for his staff. South Conway believes in helping kids to keep growing, learning, and creating opportunities for them to develop thinking and problem-solving skills. They want to educate the whole child, including their social/emotional well-being. They are on a mission to continually bring positive initiatives and conversations on campus. Their principal is intentional about creating strong and meaningful relationships with everyone on campus. Their purpose shines through in everything they do.

Gifts from the Past

Positive schools understand and appreciate the impact they have. Impact continually fuels purpose. A positive impact may be a main reason why someone chooses to enter the education profession. As you read through this section, think about the great teachers who helped you along the way. Many educators often can identify one teacher who inspired them to get into the profession. Multiple students in a class might choose to become a teacher based on their experience with a particular teacher. As a whole, the industry needs to continuously fill the pipeline of positive educators who feel called into the role and know their bigger purpose in education.

Collectively, administrators and teachers can change the direction of conversation surrounding education. They can build culture and relationships that are so strong that it will inspire a new wave of young teachers who want to enter the profession. When you live your purpose, you can have a profound and deep impact.

The recent ING Foundation study revealed 79% of students say they had a teacher who encouraged them to pursue their dreams. Students may not seek to pursue their dreams without a positive relationship with that teacher. There has to be a mutual level of trust and understanding before two people are confident and comfortable discussing dreams and future goals. This shows the influence a teacher has with a student. *Education Week* revealed students will spend 10,000 hours in a K–12 classroom over that span. Every hour and interaction count toward that student deciding what they want to do with their life and what kind of person they want to become. Think back to this "10,000-hour rule" when entering a new school year. While there are seemingly countless hours to make an impact, we start day one by setting the vision, building the relationship, and living our greater purpose.

Reinforcing the Purpose

One of the best ways to make sure educators stay rooted in purpose is to reinforce it throughout the school year. School leaders need to implement strategies at staff meetings and one-on-ones to ask teachers about their *why* and reinforce the Energy Bus rule "Drive with Purpose." At the same time, school administrators, who are usually serving many needs on campus, need to go back to their purpose too. Some leaders post their mission or purpose statement or one word on their office walls, desk, and even the background of their computer as a constant reminder to stay rooted in purpose.

Robin Fecitt, the principal at St. Joseph Catholic School in Jacksonville, Florida, believes consistency is key to success. A school that has consistent initiatives and strategies in place to handle campus needs will always be ahead of the game. Robin gave her staff plenty of lead time to read *The Energy Bus* book over summer because she was so passionate about the story and principles. She knew *The Energy Bus* could help build her campus culture. During her staff meetings she had faculty members discuss and share their purpose with each other, and she consistently reinforces their purpose.

This is a powerful practice, and we suggest that school leaders ask every staff member and teacher to talk about their own personal purpose. It is an opportunity to be vulnerable and open and share their purpose as well. This helps keep purpose alive in you and in the school. When a teacher or staff member is living their purpose through action, they should also be recognized for it. Teachers can help recognize the school administrators and staff as well when they too are living their purpose. This breeds a true community of purpose-driven educators.

Hire Purpose

Every school has a mission statement, but only the great ones have teachers and staff on a mission. When hiring teachers and staff you want to hire people who are mission-oriented and driven by purpose and then it's everyone's job to keep the purpose alive.

Purpose, mission, and vision can be included in hiring and follow-up questions for interested applicants. Tim Ridley, principal at Mt. Washington Middle School, felt the impact of the 2022–2023 school year staff shortages. It plagued thousands of schools across the country. However, Tim refused to hire "just anyone" to fill a position. He also did not get the sense from faculty that a certain position needed to be filled immediately. Others stepped up because they know their purpose is to serve students and create a positive campus culture. Tim mentioned in a monthly Certified Energy Bus for Schools coaching call that some positions had not been filled because the right person had not come along yet. Great schools hire right and hire for their culture. They hire coachable people who are rooted in purpose and mission. These individuals should be ambitious educators who are eager to serve and have a great impact on the next generation.

Purpose Helps You Thrive during Change

We must ride the waves of change. If we don't, that same wave will crash on us. If death and taxes are the only two 100% certainties in life, educators know they have a near 100% certainty that change is part of education. Every school in the country faced change when Covid hit in March 2020. Like many schools, South Conway Elementary rose up to cover student needs during this transitional period. Their teachers were resilient in staying the course to provide daily support for students and guardians who needed help. The leadership team had to work overtime to provide support and resources for staff and students to overcome this monumental challenge. It involved the entire school community rethinking how they educate students virtually.

Schools who overcame the virtual learning challenges did so because they had a unified staff that was driven by purpose and committed to student success. They knew their purpose was to educate the whole child and they had to work harder than ever to continue to engage with students. It was a unique challenge in the history of education, but purpose fuels you through every challenge, circumstance, regulation, and change. Parents from all over the country are grateful to have had creative, ambitious, dedicated, and purpose-driven teachers and staff who worked so hard to close the learning gap during that time and beyond it. While some gaps inevitably still exist due to the unique circumstances of virtual learning, students were further ahead because of the extraordinary efforts of schools with a purpose.

Desert View Middle and High School revealed they had a lot of changes entering the 2021–2022 school year, but they remained focused on their end goal. They helped to communicate to staff why the changes were happening and how they would help everyone fulfill the mission of the school. They put mission, vision, and purpose first. Even with a rocky start, their consistency and desire to help students motivated them to find their groove and create a strong culture. Jayleen Hackman, their assistant principal, admitted the school is still a work in progress but is headed in the right direction. As one of our Certified Energy Bus Schools, they have been a model of consistency for using the classroom activities guides and attending the coaching calls. They put purpose and mission first.

Change is another area that can affect students as well because anxiety and fear often accompany it. Change represents a journey into the unknown for everyone on the bus. If you trust your leaders and the passengers around you, it's a ride you are willing to take. We work with our students on discovering their purpose as part of the Certified Energy Bus for Schools program. The Energy Bus rule "Drive with Purpose" encourages students to think about this concept and how it applies to their life in an age-appropriate way.

Our middle and high school students work with "driving with purpose" on multiple levels. They are encouraged to seek their purpose in life, school, and home. We want our students to see themselves contributing to the greater good wherever they go. The teenage years provide a great opportunity for students to start exploring why they are here and what they have to offer the world. Great teachers help facilitate this process and share that life offers many possibilities. Everyone's role and actions matter.

Root Yourself in Purpose

Purpose can start with a single seed and grow and flourish into an incredible tree that is rooted in daily practices and

Students and staff learn to plant themselves right where they are.

mindsets that keeps the purpose alive. It's essential for all staff to root themselves in the school and in purpose and make the decision that this is my school! This our school. We own it!

Many of our most successful Certified Energy Bus Schools started with a single teacher handing their principal a copy of *The Energy Bus* and the principal deciding the lessons from the book would become the foundation for their culture. When the teachers rooted themselves in the principles and in their desire to live their purpose, that's when the school really experienced growth and success.

Happiness comes not from the work we do, but from how we feel about the work we do. The way we think, feel, and approach work influences our happiness at work. Educators will be happy where they decide to be happy. Where they root themselves is where they will grow and flourish. A positive school is where educators will plant themselves, get involved in committees and clubs, engage in meetings, build relationships with parents and community members, and drive the bus forward toward a great and exciting future. You can choose to be happy and engaged and work toward building a positive culture, or not. There are many things outside the control of educators, but happiness is a product of living and working with passion and purpose. You can choose to do this daily.

So get your staff on the bus and drive with purpose. Remember your why and create symbols, sayings, and reminders that help you to live and share your purpose.

These students in front of you and in your building and classrooms are your purpose—do everything possible to remember that and not forget it. When you create a fleet of purpose-driven bus drivers you will create the ride of your life.

This fleet of bus drivers is ready to create a positive vision.

Chapter 8

Create a Fleet of Bus Drivers

"It certainly is more fun on the bus," Joy said, giving George a big bright smile. He smiled back as she stepped on the gas pedal and took off to the next bus stop where someone, somewhere was waiting for the Energy Bus. They would get on and it wouldn't take long for them to learn what George now knew. The Energy Bus will surely take you on the ride of your life."

—*The Energy Bus*, page 156

Great schools are not created alone. It takes a team to build a great culture, work toward a vision, and live with a mission. It requires everyone in the school to transform negativity and fuel up with positivity and purpose. While we envision everyone at your school getting on one bus together, we also realize the key to a school's success is each individual knowing they are the driver of their bus. Each staff member and student must take the wheel and do their part to drive the bus forward. We envision your school also as a fleet of buses all moving in the same direction, excited, engaged, and driving toward a positive future!

Measuring Staff Engagement and Unity

Creating a fleet of buses is all about engagement and unity. So how do you know if you are on the right road with your staff? How do you know if they are excited, united, and engaged? Just completing a book study or being in the Energy Bus for Schools program is not enough to measure staff engagement. They both are certainly tools to head in the right direction, but staff engagement must be palpable and visible. It must be seen, felt, and heard. Heather DeBoer of Roosevelt Elementary walks around every day to check in with staff. She uses group meetings to talk about culture, curriculum, student issues, and celebrating successes of the day. Heather wants to be a presence of positivity on campus that promotes healthy and open conversations. By checking in with staff daily, she doesn't have to wait until staff meetings to hear about issues and put out fires. She receives real-time feedback every day.

Simply walking around and being present is an effective way to evaluate staff engagement and culture firsthand. We are inspired by reports of superintendents and school board members visiting campuses and talking with students and school leaders. Those making the biggest decisions for individual students and campuses need to see and feel the culture firsthand. Some schools decide to do a more formal collection of information and data. Spirit Lake Elementary is one of those schools. They created an anonymous Google Form that asks culture and climate questions about the school with a Likert scale and open-ended responses. The Likert scale has responses that measure the strength/intensity of an attitude like strongly agree, disagree, agree, and so on. Spirit Lake took these responses and then, in a supportive manner, delivered the results in staff meetings.

Nancy Kriener, the ES Lead Teacher and one of the leaders of the Energy Bus for Schools program on her campus, admitted some of the results were difficult to share and hear. However, they found that they were unaware of some problems and could now work to create solutions. Nancy recommends that school leaders seek all perspectives because it will help people to feel heard and valued. Spirit Lake is now more collectively committed to maintaining a positive environment.

When people feel seen and heard and they have the chance to weigh in, they will be more likely to buy in. Engagement surveys and questionnaires allow school leaders to collect ideas, opinions, and feedback and make improvements. Like all data, it is only as good as what you are willing to do with it. If staff is allowed to be honest and school leaders can be honest with themselves and use feedback to get better, the school will become a fleet of buses and get better together.

It's a continual process where continual growth becomes a part of your culture.

How Do You Really Know?

How do you know if culture-building initiatives are working? Ask the students. Culture is about getting everyone on the bus, and our students are a massive part of that process. We can raise the bar for them and watch them rise to it. As we know, students are very wise and often see things others miss. Getting their input is very helpful in the ongoing process of creating a fleet of bus drivers.

Below are some responses from various students at different Energy Bus Schools around the country. We asked our school leaders to have students reflect on their school's culture, the Energy Bus, and morale. Here are some of their anonymous responses:

1. Energy Bus has impacted my school and culture by showing students that being negative can have an impact on everyone.

2. Energy Bus has impacted my school culture by showing us how we should say things to each other and the impact of what we say toward other people.

3. It helped me learn to not let negative people into my life, and to go where I want to go in life rather than simply following what others want me to do.

4. Energy Bus has taught each of us about responsibility and how to be in control of your life and emotions.

5. I think it has helped people realize they should be more positive and try to be a bit more helpful.

6. Energy Bus has showed us that staying positive can not only make you feel better but can impact everyone else around you.

7. Energy Bus has helped my campus stay positive by teaching us how we can take control of our actions and life; this has helped us to take responsibility for ourselves.

8. I always try to stay positive and help others when they need it.

9. I apply Energy Bus rules to my life by staying positive and not letting Negative Nancys on my bus.

10. I use the Energy Bus rules by remembering that, if I stay positive, I can impact others by increasing positivity.

11. I stay positive and follow my own path.

12. The rule "no energy vampires" really applies to my life to pick better people to stay in my life.

It is apparent that these responses show connected and engaged students. When schools spend valuable resources and time to invest in culture and relationships, they will see the results and when they ask for and receive feedback they get better. School leaders collected some of the above responses with small group meetings, surveys, and one-on-ones. The Energy Bus for Schools program has never had a school come to us and say, "It didn't work." If you build it, drive it, and help others take the wheel, great things happen.

Dr. Jim Van Allan doing a student assembly.

Families are a Part of the Fleet!

Imagine if you polled 100 parents at your school and asked them, what are some brands, companies, or organizations you feel an emotional attachment to? How many of them would say their child's school? How many teachers or staff would say the school as well? We have emotional attachments to teams, products, clothes, and celebrities, but what about the things most personal to us? Our community and schools matter significantly. A study by the Association for Consumer Research revealed that consumers who are attached to brands report feeling affectionate toward, passionate about, and connected to that brand. They show an intense loyalty to the brand and will often pay a premium for it as well.

We may not look at our parents as consumers, but there are now many choices in the education system. Parents can send their children to public, charter, private, religious, sports, virtual, trade, and other types of schools for K–12 education. Homeschooling is an important option to look at as well. The National Home Education Research Institute revealed that there are almost 3.135 million school-aged (K–12) homeschool students in the United States as of 2022. Many school districts have even instituted school choice where parents can pick which school their child attends.

Schools must continually strive for excellence in culture, leadership, communication, and relationship to attract not only the best teachers, but students, parents, and families. Parents and families are a part of your culture and you want to include and involve them to be bus drivers with you. Highly invested parents will serve on boards, volunteer, raise money, run the PTA, and help the school immensely.

Creating Connection

Many of the examples shared in this book reveal a blueprint for building connections to the school and to each other. School leaders connect with their staff. The staff connects with each other and their students. A connected school then connects with parents and invites them to be part of their culture and growth process. Together everyone creates a dynamic and thriving school community.

Parents visiting the campus, volunteering for events, and leading many initiatives creates engagement, buy-in, and unity. They see and feel the school and now feel like they are a part of it. They become invested because they see themselves as part of the solution. This adds to the collective belief. Students also should feel proud of their environment. School spirit days, sporting events, and extracurriculars should be encouraged. Academics alone are not enough to build immense school pride and emotional connections. A strong bond with the school may motivate the student to accomplish success, not just for themselves but for the school community as well.

What's Next?

You've created a fleet of buses! Congrats! What's next? Many schools will reach a point where they know a positive transformation has occurred. However, as Leon Hayes at South Conway Elementary put it, that is not the end of the story. Teachers, staff, and students need to be continuous leaders and learners. Continuous training and strategic professional development to keep growing and never give up is always essential.

Roosevelt Elementary believes that constant contagious positivity is still necessary, even after a positive culture is built. It takes time, energy, and focus, but if you let go of this commitment, the positivity can slip. Once a collective positivity is reached, each staff member and student must continually look for ways to grow and share positivity with others. If everyone sees themselves as part of the solution and success, they will keep driving the bus forward. Circumstances may change and the world may change but the vision, mission, and positivity should never change.

When positivity and belief is the norm, everything runs better. Our fleet of bus drivers will be on a mission: unstoppable forces with the goal to keep learning, growing, and improving. What's next is simple: keep learning with a growth mindset. A staff needs to collectively decide how much effort they want to put into learning new classroom and teaching strategies, team-building activities, and relational development. Just because a staff member has been at the school or in education for 30 years does not mean they cannot learn something new. Some of our best audience members in school trainings and workshops are those with the most experience in the field. They want to keep learning and growing so they can perform at optimal levels throughout the year. It is also a significant way to pass on knowledge to new staff members. No matter your experience as an educator or level of success as a school, a growth mindset is essential.

Colleyville Middle School

Colleyville Middle School in Dallas, Texas, has received almost every accolade available for a school. Their principal, Dr. David Arencibia, won the Texas Secondary Principal of the Year and was a top-three finalist for national principal of the year. The National PTA School of Excellence considers them an A-rated school. It was no surprise to hear that Dr. Arencibia used *The Power of a Positive Team* and *The Energy Bus* on campus to help drive school culture. They are also a Certified Energy Bus School. Despite their success, they still believe they can get better and are always looking for ideas to do so. We are honored to be part of their growth going forward. They know the journey has just begun because it is harder to stay on top than to reach the top. If your school or district is flying high, this may be the best time to invest in culture.

In the beginning of this book, we discussed the importance of core values and knowing what they stand for to build a positive school culture. Colleyville's mission is to be the best and to build an excellent school together. They identify their core values as positivity, strengths, team, and growth mindset. Dr. Arencibia makes it clear, and they are reinforced in all meetings and communication. By knowing and reinforcing the values, they are building a fleet of bus drivers who hold each other accountable to that mission. With clarity of vision, they create effective systems that support their positive culture. One system is the hiring process. They have refined the interview process to ask specific questions and look for incoming staff who will positively contribute to the mission in a positive and engaging way.

Another system that defines their culture is the consistent practice of reflection and collaboration. When decisions need to be made, the input of staff is considered. Colleyville's collaborative culture is all about expectations of the behavior and actions they want to see. Their school leadership works hard to clearly communicate the expectations and the justifications for them. Part of their weekly meetings as school leaders is to reflect on what is working, what is not working, and what can improve. These reflective practices allow them to adjust to staff and environmental changes that inevitably happen throughout the year.

Colleyville Middle School clearly has a positive, engaging, and collaborative school culture. Their principal made it clear they were not done yet and always want to focus on continuous improvement. Even though they have mastered many of the main concepts found in this book, there is still a significant drive to get better. They do not want to rest on past success. They know that by taking their eyes off the goal of "being the best," negativity and apathy can begin to set in. They do not want to wait for success to happen; they want to work for it so it becomes inevitable.

One key line that Dr. Arencibia told us is that "You can literally feel the positive school environment when you enter the building and interact with staff and students." That palpable feeling is the result of the contribution everyone has made to create the campus culture. If you want to work at Colleyville Middle School, the expectation is you want to contribute to the positive culture and see yourself as part of the success. They provide fun activities like BBQ lunches, drink carts, book studies, thank-you cards, and teacher lounge treats as part of the greater strategy to enhance that "positive feeling" when you come onto campus. The Energy Bus has been a true source of inspiration for them on what a campus culture should be focused on. They are all driving their fleet of buses as the Energy Bus rolls on!

The Best Is Yet to Come

The preface to this book focused on my (Jim's) story about meeting Jon and launching *The Energy Bus*. Many of your school stories started with picking up that book or another Jon Gordon title. We know culture takes work and books, programs, and speakers can aid in school development. Our Energy Bus for Schools mission is "to develop positive school leaders and educators who positively impact students and create a more positive world." We work to live this mission daily.

Colleyville Middle School is fully aboard the Energy Bus.

Educators are working in the most challenging era in modern history. Sometimes it's hard to believe that the best is yet to come. It can be even harder to remain positive on campus when negativity and challenges always come your way. It is easy to blame and point fingers for certain aspects of the education system; however, your students will still be coming to campus every day. Their smiles, laughter, and energy will fill the halls and classrooms. They will be looking to teachers and administrators for how to act and respond to adversity in this world. What an opportunity every day to reach these students and make sure they feel loved, supported, encouraged, and inspired. It won't always be easy, but no one entered the education field thinking it would be easy. If you are reading this, you feel called into the profession. You are meant to be here. You are meant to have an impact. Your belief, positivity, and purpose must be greater than any negativity or challenge out there. You can't control all the things happening in your city, state, and community regarding budgets, politics, and current events, but you can control what you do every day in your school building and classrooms. Be sure to stay positive and continue to make a difference! Our students and communities need our schools to become destination locations, places where people want to work and students want to attend. The phrase "The best is yet to come" means we never stop the journey of improvement. So hop on the Energy Bus and let's enjoy the ride of our lives while creating great schools together.

ENERGY BUS
for SCHOOLS
Create a Positive School Culture
THE ENERGY BUS
THE ENERGY BUS
JON GORDON
10 Rules to Fuel Your Life, Work, and Team with Positive Energy

What's Next for Your School or District?

1. Become a Certified Energy Bus School

We give you the blueprint and framework to create a great culture, energize teachers and students, and transform negativity. Schools and districts are given resources and tools to implement *The Energy Bus* on campus in a fun and interactive way. There are grade-level-appropriate activity guides for classrooms, monthly group coaching for school leaders, and resources for staff to connect to *The Energy Bus* rules. Best of all, you'll join a community of schools and school leaders who share best practices with each other. Please visit www.EnergyBusSchools.com for more information or scan the QR code below.

2. Become a Certified Speaker/Trainer for the Energy Bus for Schools Program

If you have ever wanted to become a speaker or workshop leader, this is the training program for our educators. You will be given the license and resources to use the Energy Bus for Schools workshop and training materials in order to impact schools. This train-the-trainer virtual session will equip you with the resources needed to become a successful education speaker as a Certified Energy Bus for Schools Speaker/Trainer. This is the perfect opportunity for those who want to deliver workshops within their district as an employee or become an independent speaker/trainer who works with schools around the country. Please visit www.EnergyBusSchools.com or scan the QR code below.

3. Bring the Energy Bus to Your Campus with a Book Study and Speaking Engagement

Please contact us at info@JonGordon.com for information on bulk book orders for *The Energy Bus* and *The Energy Bus for Schools*. A staff book study provides a unique experience to discover the principles from the book together and create the foundation for a positive campus culture. A speaking engagement by Dr. Jim Van Allan and other members of the Energy Bus for Schools speaking team provides a highly interactive experience that brings *the Energy Bus* to life. With thought-provoking discussions, engaging activities, and practical strategies, an external voice may be what your school or district needs to elevate your culture.

4. Positive Educator Newsletter

For ongoing strategies and resources to help energize your school culture and to stay up to date on all Energy Bus for Schools offerings and opportunities, please visit www.energybusschools.com/newsletter to receive our free monthly newsletter or scan the QR code below.

BECOME A CERTIFIED TRAINER AND SPEAKER

Live your Purpose and Make a Greater Impact

Deliver Speeches and Workshops based on *The Energy Bus / The Energy Bus for Schools* books!

When you become a Certified Energy Bus for Schools Trainer and Speaker, we'll teach and equip you with all the tools you need to deliver workshops and keynotes based on *The Energy Bus*. This is perfect for staff within a school / district or for speakers / coaches who want to build their own speaking / training business and impact multiple schools.

Acknowledgments

Dr. Jim Van Allan

First, I would like to thank my wife, Stephanie, for the endless encouragement and support in the writing process. I hope this book can be a light for my children to follow their dreams and work to have a positive impact on our world.

Thank you to the schools I attended growing up in Palm Harbor, Florida (Sutherland Elementary, Palm Harbor Middle School, and Palm Harbor University High School), for giving me an incredible experience as a student. I am the speaker and man today because of great schools and even better teachers.

Thank you to Jon Gordon for the opportunity to help co-author this book and be the president of The Energy Bus for Schools program. It's been an amazing journey from intern to president, and I am grateful for the ongoing support, mentorship, and friendship since we met in 2006. I know our teamwork with this book will impact so many educators out there. Speaking of educators, know that you are loved and appreciated. Jon Gordon and I love our educators and will do anything to support you. Thank you for dedicating your lives to service.

Jon Gordon

I would like to thank Jim Van Allan for all his hard work and dedication to helping school leaders and educators rise up to their potential. I would like to thank him for his commitment to the principles and messages of *The Energy Bus* ever since he was a college student. To see the leader and difference maker he has become is inspiring.

I would also like to thank all the educators who have embraced *The Energy Bus* and utilized it to help your students and school improve. I have loved watching you shine and see you share your genius over the years. You are my heroes!

About the Authors

Jon Gordon has inspired millions of readers around the world. He is the author of 28 books, including five children's books and 15 bestsellers: *The Energy Bus, The Carpenter, Training Camp, You Win in the Locker Room First, The Power of Positive Leadership, The Power of a Positive Team, The Coffee Bean, Stay Positive, The Garden, Relationship Grit, Stick Together, Row the Boat,* and *The Sale*. He is passionate about developing positive leaders, organizations, and teams. Visit him at JonGordon.com.

Dr. Jim Van Allan is the president of The Energy Bus for Schools program, which gives schools the blueprint and framework to create a positive school culture. He coaches school leaders and superintendents on mindset, teamwork, communication, and culture-building. Additionally, Jim speaks to schools and districts across the country with keynotes, trainings, workshops, and student assemblies.

Jim is also a professor of communication studies and lead speech instructor with Keiser University, which is based in Florida. He teaches public speaking, interpersonal communication, and business communication.

Jim holds a bachelor of science in public relations from the University of Florida and a master of arts in communication studies from Florida Atlantic University. He also earned his PhD in education leadership from Keiser University.

For Jim's dissertation research, he studied the impact of an early version of The Energy Bus for Schools program on a model school in Ohio. Much of his research centered around the impact of sustainable professional development for schools.

He runs The Energy Bus for Schools podcast and helps with a charity YouTube channel called *The Fitness Mission*. Jim lives in Palm City, Florida, with his wife and three children, Brady, Brenden, and Brinley. You can follow him on social media @JimVanAllan on all platforms.

Other Books by Jon Gordon

The Energy Bus

A man whose life and career are in shambles learns from a unique bus driver and set of passengers how to overcome adversity. Enjoy an enlightening ride of positive energy that is improving the way leaders lead, employees work, and teams function.
www.TheEnergyBus.com

The No Complaining Rule

Follow a vice president of human resources who must save herself and her company from ruin and discover proven principles and an actionable plan to win the battle against individual and organizational negativity.
www.NoComplainingRule.com

Training Camp

This inspirational story about a small guy with a big heart, and a special coach who guides him on a quest for excellence, reveals the 11 winning habits that separate the best individuals and teams from the rest.
www.TrainingCamp11.com

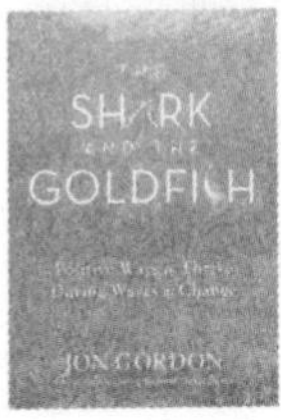

The Shark and the Goldfish

Delightfully illustrated, this quick read is packed with tips and strategies on how to respond to challenges beyond your control in order to thrive during waves of change.
www.SharkandGoldfish.com

Soup

The newly appointed CEO of a popular soup company is brought in to reinvigorate the brand and bring success back to a company that has fallen on hard times. Through her journey, discover the key ingredients to unite, engage, and inspire teams to create a culture of greatness.
www.Soup11.com

The Seed

Go on a quest for the meaning and passion behind work with Josh, an up-and-comer at his company who is disenchanted with his job. Through Josh's cross-country journey, you'll find surprising new sources of wisdom and inspiration in your own business and life.
www.Seed11.com

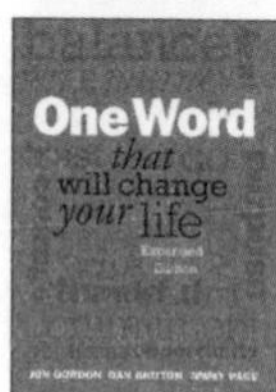

One Word

One Word is a simple concept that delivers powerful life change! This quick read will inspire you to simplify your life and work by focusing on just one word for this year. *One Word* creates clarity, power, passion, and life-change. When you find your word, live it, and share it, your life will become more rewarding and exciting than ever.
www.getoneword.com

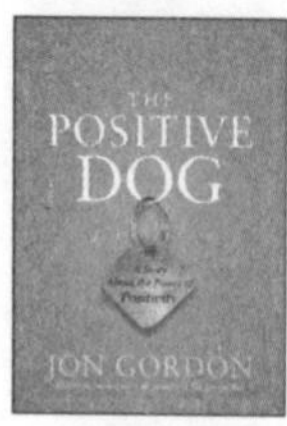

The Positive Dog

We all have two dogs inside of us. One dog is positive, happy, optimistic, and hopeful. The other dog is negative, mad, pessimistic, and fearful. These two dogs often fight inside us, but guess who wins? The one you feed the most. *The Positive Dog* is an inspiring story that not only reveals the strategies and benefits of being positive, but also an essential truth: being positive doesn't just make you better; it makes everyone around you better.
www.feedthepositivedog.com

The Carpenter

The Carpenter is Jon Gordon's most inspiring book yet—filled with powerful lessons and success strategies. Michael wakes up in the hospital with a bandage on his head and fear in his heart after collapsing during a morning jog. When Michael finds out the man who saved his life is a carpenter, he visits him and quickly learns that he is more than just a carpenter; he is also a builder of lives, careers, people, and teams. In this journey, you will learn timeless principles to help you stand out, excel, and make an impact on people and the world.

www.carpenter11.com

The Hard Hat

A true story about Cornell lacrosse player George Boiardi, *The Hard Hat* is an unforgettable book about a selfless, loyal, joyful, hard-working, competitive, and compassionate leader and teammate, the impact he had on his team and program, and the lessons we can learn from him. This inspirational story will teach you how to build a great team and be the best teammate you can be.

www.hardhat21.com

You Win in the Locker Room First

Based on the extraordinary experiences of NFL Coach Mike Smith and leadership expert Jon Gordon, *You Win in the Locker Room First* offers a rare, behind-the-scenes look at one of the most pressure-packed leadership jobs on the planet, and what leaders can learn from these experiences in order to build their own winning teams.

www.winninthelockerroom.com

Life Word

Life Word reveals a simple, powerful tool to help you identify the word that will inspire you to live your best life while leaving your greatest legacy. In the process, you'll discover your *why*, which will help show you how to live with a renewed sense of power, purpose, and passion.

www.getoneword.com/lifeword

The Power of Positive Leadership

The Power of Positive Leadership is your personal coach for becoming the leader your people deserve. Jon Gordon gathers insights from his bestselling fables to bring you the definitive guide to positive leadership. Difficult times call for leaders who are up to the challenge. Results are the by-product of your culture, teamwork, vision, talent, innovation, execution, and commitment. This book shows you how to bring it all together to become a powerfully positive leader.

www.powerofpositiveleadership.com

The Power of a Positive Team

In *The Power of a Positive Team*, Jon Gordon draws on his unique team-building experience, as well as conversations with some of the greatest teams in history, to provide an essential framework of proven practices to empower teams to work together more effectively and achieve superior results.

www.PowerOfAPositiveTeam.com

The Coffee Bean

From bestselling author Jon Gordon and rising star Damon West comes *The Coffee Bean*: an illustrated fable that teaches readers how to transform their environment, overcome challenges, and create positive change.

www.coffeebeanbook.com

Stay Positive

Fuel yourself and others with positive energy—inspirational quotes and encouraging messages to live by from bestselling author, Jon Gordon. Keep this little book by your side, read from it each day, and feed your mind, body, and soul with the power of positivity.

www.StayPositiveBook.com

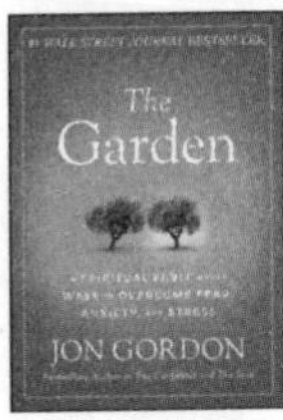

The Garden

The Garden is an enlightening and encouraging fable that helps readers overcome the 5 D's (doubt, distortion, discouragement, distractions, and division) in order to find more peace, focus, connection, and happiness. Jon tells a story of teenage twins who, through the help of a neighbor and his special garden, find ancient wisdom, life-changing lessons, and practical strategies to overcome the fear, anxiety, and stress in their lives.

www.readthegarden.com

Relationship Grit

Bestselling author Jon Gordon is back with another life-affirming book. This time, he teams up with Kathryn Gordon, his wife of 23 years, for a look at what it takes to build strong relationships. In *Relationship Grit*, the Gordons reveal what brought them together, what kept them together through difficult times, and what continues to sustain their love and passion for one another to this day.

www.relationshipgritbook.com

Stick Together

From bestselling author Jon Gordon and coauthor Kate Leavell, *Stick Together* delivers a crucial message about the power of belief, ownership, connection, love, inclusion, consistency, and hope. The authors guide individuals and teams on an inspiring journey to show them how to persevere through challenges, overcome obstacles, and create success together.

www.sticktogetherbook.com

Row the Boat

In *Row the Boat*, Minnesota Golden Gophers Head Coach P.J. Fleck and bestselling author Jon Gordon deliver an inspiring message about what you can achieve when you approach life with a never-give-up philosophy. The book shows you how to choose enthusiasm and optimism as your guiding lights instead of being defined by circumstances and events outside of your control.
www.rowtheboatbook.com

The Sale

In *The Sale*, bestselling author Jon Gordon and rising star Alex Demczak deliver an invaluable lesson about what matters most in life and work and how to achieve it. The book teaches four lessons about integrity in order to create lasting success.
www.thesalebook.com

The One Word Journal

In *The One Word Journal*, bestselling authors Jon Gordon, Dan Britton, and Jimmy Page deliver a powerful new approach to simplifying and transforming your life and business. You'll learn how to access the core of your intention every week of the year as you explore 52 weekly lessons, principles, and wins that unleash the power of your One Word.

How to Be a Coffee Bean

In *How to Be a Coffee Bean*, bestselling coauthors of *The Coffee Bean*, Jon Gordon and Damon West, present 111 simple and effective strategies to help you lead a coffee bean lifestyle—one full of healthy habits, encouragement, and genuine happiness. From athletes to students and executives, countless individuals have been inspired by *The Coffee Bean* message. Now, *How to Be a Coffee Bean* teaches you how to put *The Coffee Bean* philosophy into action to help you create real and lasting change in your life.

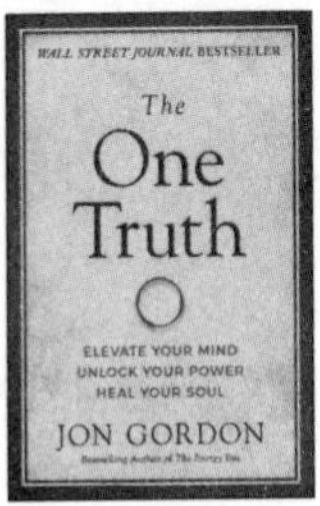

The One Truth

In *The One Truth*, bestselling author and thought leader Jon Gordon guides you on a path to discover revolutionary insights, ancient truths, and practical strategies to elevate your mind, unlock your power, and live life to the fullest. Once you know the One Truth, you'll see how it impacts leadership, teamwork, mindset, performance, relationships, addictions, social media, anxiety, mental health, healing, and ultimately determines what you create and experience.

The Energy Bus for Kids

The illustrated children's adaptation of the bestselling book *The Energy Bus* tells the story of George, who, with the help of his school bus driver, Joy, learns that if he believes in himself, he'll find the strength to overcome any challenge. His journey teaches kids how to overcome negativity, bullies, and everyday challenges to be their best.

www.EnergyBusKids.com

Thank You and Good Night

Thank You and Good Night is a beautifully illustrated book that shares the heart of gratitude. Jon Gordon takes a little boy and girl on a fun-filled journey from one perfect moonlit night to the next. During their adventurous days and nights, the children explore the people, places, and things they are thankful for.

The Hard Hat for Kids

The Hard Hat for Kids is an illustrated guide to teamwork. Adapted from the bestseller *The Hard Hat*, this uplifting story presents practical insights and life-changing lessons that are immediately applicable to everyday situations, giving kids—and adults—a new outlook on cooperation, friendship, and the selfless nature of true teamwork.

www.HardHatforKids.com

One Word for Kids

If you could choose only one word to help you have your best year ever, what would it be? *Love? Fun? Believe? Brave?* It's probably different for each person. How you find your word is just as important as the word itself. And once you know your word, what do you do with it? In *One Word for Kids,* bestselling author Jon Gordon—along with coauthors Dan Britton and Jimmy Page—asks these questions to children and adults of all ages, teaching an important life lesson in the process.

www.getoneword.com/kids

The Coffee Bean for Kids

The bestselling authors of *The Coffee Bean* inspire and encourage children with this transformative tale of personal strength. Perfect for parents, teachers, and children who wish to overcome negativity and challenging situations, *The Coffee Bean for Kids* teaches readers about the potential that each one of us has to lead, influence, and make a positive impact on others and the world.

www.coffeebeankidsbook.com

Index